Each year The New York Public Library and Oxford University Press invite a prominent figure in the arts and letters to give a series of lectures on a topic of his or her choice. The lectures become the basis of a book jointly published by the Library and the Press. The previous books in the series are *The Old World's New World* by C. Vann Woodward, *Culture of Complaint: The Fraying of America* by Robert Hughes, and *Witches and Jesuits: Shakespeare's Macbeth* by Garry Wills.

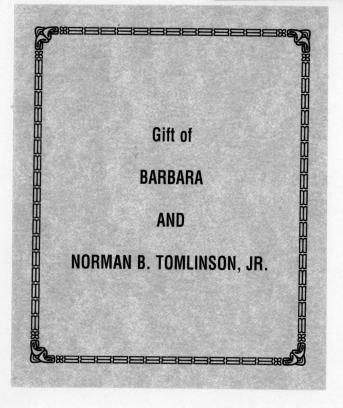

Vis

o

Fu

Visions

OF THE

Future

The Distant Past, Yesterday, Today, Tomorrow

ROBERT HEILBRONER

The New York Public Library
OXFORD UNIVERSITY PRESS
New York   Oxford
1995

Oxford University Press

Oxford   New York
Athens   Auckland   Bangkok   Bombay
Calcutta   Cape Town   Dar es Salaam   Delhi
Florence   Hong Kong   Istanbul   Karachi
Kuala Lumpur   Madras   Madrid   Melbourne
Mexico City   Nairobi   Paris   Singapore
Taipei   Tokyo   Toronto

and associated companies in
Berlin   Ibadan

#30737537

Copyright © 1995 by Robert Heilbroner

Published jointly by The New York Public Library and
Oxford University Press, Inc.

Oxford is a registered trademark of Oxford University Press

The name "The New York Public Library" is a registered trademark
and the property of The New York Public Library,
Astor, Lenox and Tilden Foundations

Library of Congress Cataloging-in-Publication Data
Heilbroner, Robert L.
Visions of the future :
the distant past, yesterday, today, tomorrow /
Robert Heilbroner.
p. cm.   Based on a series of lectures.
Includes bibliographical references and index.
ISBN 0-19-509074-8
1. Forecasting—History.
2. Civilization, Modern—20th century—Philosophy.
I. Title.   CB158.H39   1995
303.49'09'03—dc20   94-21635

9 8 7 6 5 4 3 2 1

Printed in the United States of America
on acid free paper

For David Gordon

Acknowledgments

This book is the fruit of an unexpected, and all the more deeply appreciated, joint invitation from the New York Public Library and the Oxford University Press to give three lectures on a subject of my choice, the lectures to become the basis for a short book. I hope the pages that follow will continue the broad, humanistic purposes of my predecessors in this series, C. Vann Woodward, Robert Hughes, and Gary Wills.

I am grateful to Edward Barry, President of Oxford University Press, and to David Cronin, of the New York Public Library, for having made this undertaking possible, and to Peter Bernstein, Stanley Burnshaw, Eli Sagan, Aaron Singer, William Milberg, and my wife, Shirley, who read the manuscript with scrupulous care. I owe them a great debt.

One further introductory remark seems warranted. In a work of this scope, substantiation becomes a hopeless problem. A volume twice this size would be needed to provide scholarly evidence to underpin what I have written; and another book, twice that size, to defend my choice of references. On the other hand, it seems wrong to present bold theses without a shred of supporting argument. I have tried to steer a middle course by providing enough citations to satisfy the curious, but not so many as to suggest omniscience. Like so many other middle courses, this one may end up satisfying no one, but at least the reader will know that I have thought hard about the problem, however unsuccessfully I may have resolved it.

Contents

Visions

OF THE

Future

1
PREVIEW

I

This is an exceedingly long, short book, stretching
from archeological beginnings 150,000 years in the
past to who knows how many millennia into the future.
Hence, it may be helpful to begin by setting the project into
perspective. I have written more than once about the shape
of things to come, to use H. G. Wells's wonderful title that
conjures up the future as an imagined landscape seen from
afar. Much of that writing has recounted how the great
economists foresaw the prospective landscapes of their
times—Adam Smith, for example, envisaging a future of
economic growth accompanied by the intellectual and moral
decay of the laboring class (the latter not often mentioned
when we speak of Smith's vision)[1] Karl Marx projecting a
drama of a self-destructive capitalism laying the basis for the
constructive tasks of socialism.

These remarkable scenarios perhaps have been the
most significant accomplishment of economics, not because
any of them turned out to be wholly prescient, but for a
reason of which I suspect their originators were unaware: to
provide a plausible framework within which to face that

most fearsome of psychological necessities—looking into the future. As we study and compare these bold projections, their rightness and wrongness fade in importance before their ministration to this common need. By enabling us to see our lives as part of a great collective journeying toward some destination, however indistinct, the works of the worldly philosophers offer some kind of consolation for the all too clearly foreseeable destination of each member of the collectivity, which is death.

I do not start with the narratives of the great economists to place them at the center of this book. On the contrary, they serve my purpose precisely because they stand out as extraordinary exceptions to numberless conceptions of the future in which—with a stunning instance to which we will come in due course—the shape of things to come is indistinguishable from the shape of things at hand. Indeed, it is the virtual absence of social scenarios of any kind within the vast sweep of the past that makes it possible to assert the credulity-straining premise on which my book rests, namely that humanity's worldly expectations can be described rather simply. Despite the enormous range of societal organization, technological development, and cultural achievement that characterize what we know, or can reasonably divine, of the past, I suggest we can find no more than three distinct visions of the future over its entire extent. For brevity's sake, I shall call them the visions of the Distant Past, of Yesterday, and of Today, which includes some portion of Tomorrow.

By the Distant Past, I refer to all of human existence from the appearance of Homo sapiens 150,000 years ago down to Yesterday, which begins a mere two or three hun-

dred years ago. To depict this immense panorama as consti-
tuting a single chapter of history seems hopelessly Procrus-
tean and will appear even more so as we consider what it
includes. The Distant Past begins with primitive societies
dependent for at least a hundred thousand years on stone and
flint implements, followed by ten to twenty thousand years
during which the gradient of material change slowly tilts
upward with the use of copper and bronze, to be followed,
in turn, starting perhaps in the sixth millennium B.C., by the
scaling of a great escarpment of social change—a feat that
itself lasted several thousand years—atop which were established the first complexly stratified societies of history, the
Mesopotamian, Egyptian, Indian, and Chinese kingdoms
and empires. Thereafter, the Distant Past goes on to include
the glory that was Greece and the grandeur that was Rome,
the political confusion of the Middle Ages, and finally the
appearance of the modern nation-state in Europe in the seventeenth century, during all of which time we can find in
Asia civilizations superior in technology, social organization, and culture to those of the West.

Thus, our first period is marked by an enormous range
of diversity in virtually every aspect of life, except one: its
view of the earthly future. Moreover, the unifying aspect of
that view can be described simply. The seers of the primitive
tribes and communities that occupy the overwhelming bulk
of the Distant Past, and the oracles and priests who advised
the rulers of its later kingdoms and empires, looked into the
future to discern every aspect of the shape of things to come
but one—the material prospects for the larger society to
which they belonged.

Weather, the great regulator of agriculture, was beyond

all prognostication. With very few exceptions, the tools and techniques of production remained the same from one generation to the next. Economic historians have often remarked that a horse collar enabling an animal to pull a cart without choking itself was not developed in the West until the thirteenth century. Except for trickles of "foreign" trade, economic life, insofar as it was distinguishable from social life in general, was a force for stasis, not for change. At the very apex of the first stratified societies, dynastic dreams were dreamt and visions of triumph or ruin entertained; but there is no mention in the papyri and cuneiform tablets on which these hopes and fears were recorded that they envisaged, in the slightest degree, changes in the material conditions of the great masses of the people, or for that matter, of the ruling class itself.

These ubiquitously encountered expectations of changelessness concern the material outlook of the Distant Past—the range and quality of goods that determined its everyday way of life, its "standard of living." But there was also another unifying element in its visions of the non-material, religious world. Here again, at first glance we are struck by the variety of what we find—the vague spiritlike afterlife that seems to have been the form taken by religion in the earliest hunting and gathering societies, the various permutations of reincarnation found in many Eastern cultures, salvation and damnation in the Christian era. Yet, once more, there seems to be a common thread. It is that all these mystical or religious visions can be seen as posthumous rewards or punishments, not as foretastes of possibilities for life on earth. Thus, throughout the vast extent and varied forms of the Distant Past, religion serves as consolation for a changelessness that is beyond reach or hope in its earlier societies, or as a warning against violating codes of behavior, which in all later societies preach the acceptance of things as they have always been and must always remain.

Hence, from long before the Lascaux caves to the time of Isaac Newton and the fall of the Ming Dynasty in the seventeenth century, the shape of things to come, insofar as it concerned the conditions of existence for the unborn descendants of existing society, was assumed to be a matter hidden behind an impenetrable veil of ignorance. It was, of course, also the case that for the vast majorities of these societies, this ignorance was reinforced by impotence: what could simple peasants do to change their material prospects? Yet, matters were not too different at the apex of these societies, where, at first sight, imperial power would seem to have constituted a major force capable of altering the future. Certainly the rulers of Sumer and Akkad, of Shang China and imperial Rome, of Spain in Columbus's time, and England in Shakespeare's were all engaged in ceaseless efforts to expand their realms or to defend them against incursions from rival empires; and all sought to leave behind enduring monuments, of which the pyramids of pharaohonic Egypt are only the best-known examples.

Such ambitious engagements with the future seem light-years removed from the resignation of the masses of the populace. Yet even at these imperial levels we can find a common element that links their visions of the future to those of humble rank. It is the absence of any sense that great impersonal forces could be counted on as allies in their undertakings. Kings, pharaohs, emperors, warlords, and re-

9

ligious leaders launched their ventures with whatever assurance could be given by alliances, treaties, and superiorities of arms, not to mention sacrifices to the gods or a firm reliance on God's will, but they could not do so with the confidence that massive self-generated changes, as powerful as the silting up of rivers or the erosion of shorelines, would be on their side.

The reason, of course, is that there were no such self-generated changes—at least none that could be reliably anticipated. Moreover, none would come into being until the appearance of the social equivalents of natural forces—an event that would take place behind the backs of, or in utter indifference to the knowledge, efforts, or wishes of peasants, kings, or priests alike. In their power to rearrange the possibilities of daily life, the new agencies of change were similar to the silting up of rivers or the erosion of shorelines, but they were different in that they sprang from social life itself, rather than descending on it from suprahuman realms. One of these forces was the penetration of new technologies and knowledge into the routines of daily economic life. Another was the appearance of social and political currents that altered norms from static custom to generational change, not only in the look and style of things, but in the vocabulary of social and political ideas. Along with these changes, the fixity and impenetrability that had characterized all views of the future over the vast span of the Distant Past come to an end. A new chapter begins, to which I have given the name Yesterday, but which is more accurately described as the rise and flourishing of capitalism, with its sister forces of technology and science and of an emerging political consciousness.

II

Yesterday is the period in which our forebears grew up and most of us have come of age. It is perhaps best imagined as commencing in the time of our great-great grandparents' great-great grandparents, and lasting until a boundary drawn in recent years, perhaps between the end of World War II and the collapse of the Soviet Union. More important, it is the age from which we are only now emerging, if I am correct in believing that a new appraisal of the shape of the future is emerging in our own time.

But we have not yet described that which leads us to place Yesterday's 250-odd years—from roughly the beginning of the eighteenth century until the second half of the twentieth—in a class by themselves, decisively differentiated from the countless thousands of years that preceded, and the tiny few that have followed them. We have already begun to see the answer in the institutional changes that separated the two eras, but I have not yet said the words that make the crucial difference. It is that the future now enters into human consciousness as a great beckoning prospect.

At the lower levels of society as well as in its uppermost echelons, the shape of things to come assumes a new guise, as the carrier of previously unimaginable possibilities for improving the human condition at all levels. From what Adam Smith called "an augmentation of fortune," through the ability to command hitherto untamable forces of nature. Yesterday denotes an era in which we look to the future with confidence, because men and women believe that forces will be working there for their betterment, both as individuals and as a collectivity. We shall wait until the chapter following the next to examine those forces in more detail, and to consider the changes they were expected to generate in the human condition. For the moment, it is enough if I have made plausible that so brief a moment in history deserves to be given a degree of weight in an inquiry into visions of the future, equal to or greater than that of all the millennia that preceded it.

There is, however, one very important characteristic of the period I call Yesterday that distinguishes it from the Distant Future. Unlike that earlier era in which the future everywhere looked the same because nowhere was it seen as a repository of powerful secular improvements, Yesterday's view of the future appears differently in different parts of the political globe. Harnessed as it was to the propulsive effects of capitalism, science, and popular political movements, it manifests itself almost entirely in those portions of the world in which these forces established themselves most firmly, which is to say, in what we call the West. Elsewhere—in Africa, most of Asia, Latin America, and the more backward parts of Europe—the material conditions of the Distant Past continued unchanged, and the future remained more or less as it had always been, without any perceived dynamics whose workings would advance the condition of all.

Thus, the change in expectations regarding what lay ahead was largely confined to Western Europe and Northern America, with a few outposts elsewhere, such as the Antipodes. Yesterday therefore remained, for almost all its two and a half centuries, an amalgam of two periods, in which the inertia of the Distant Past continued to form the expectations of the greater bulk of humanity, while the conditions of a new era lifted the hopes of those who lived in the handful of nations for whom the decisive page in history's book had been turned.

III

These matters, like a number of others, must await our further scrutiny at the appropriate time, but there still remains the last and most important period—the one in which we live. Today's vision of the future is certainly not that of the Distant Past, for if there was ever a time in which the shape of things to come was seen as dominated by impersonal forces, it is ours. Science, economics, mass political movements—the three most powerful carriers of those future-shaping influences—are the stuff of everyday headlines. What differentiates them from those of Yesterday is that they now appear as potentially or even actively malign, as well as benign; both as threatening and supportive, ominous as well as reassuring even in the most favored nations—that is, the most fully capitalist, science-oriented, and politically democratic. Indeed, it is precisely in those nations that the vision of the future has been most perceptibly altered.

We will not explore this change of expectations in any depth until we reach our last chapters, but in this first overview it must be already apparent that the conclusions at which I shall arrive cannot enjoy the same degree of historical support that I hope to provide for what precedes them. I must therefore spend the last words of this Preview acknowledging the contestability of the vision of Today.

Here I shall take as a countertext an analysis of world

prospects, *The Real World Order: Zones of Peace/ Zones of Turmoil,*[2] by Max Singer and the late Aaron Wildavsky, two respected political analysts. Their basic premise is clearly laid out at the beginning of Chapter 1:

The key to understanding the real world order is to separate the world into two parts. One part is zones of peace, wealth, and democracy. The other part is zones of turmoil, war, and development. There are useful things to say about the zones of peace; and there are useful things to say about the zones of turmoil, but if you try to talk about the world as a whole all you get is falsehood or platitudes.[3]

Singer and Wildavsky have many insightful things to say about the differences between these zones, although their assessment approaches the larger question from a perspective considerably different from my own. As an example, I have not been able to find in their text the word "capitalism," in which I lay great store with respect to the historic implications of our own times. More germane to our present purposes, Singer's and Wildavsky's intention is to counter the "fashionable pessimism" that they see as characteristic of the moment.[4] Appropriately, their book is dedicated to the memory of Herman Kahn, a futurist of the 1960s and 1970s, well known for his bold, often unorthdox, and largely positive views of coming events.[5] Saluting their mentor, Singer and Wildavsky write ". . . he would have gloried in the world's brilliant prospects." The thrust of their own view is clearly set forth in the opening paragraphs of their Introduction:

Whether this book is optimistic or pessimistic depends on whether a century is a short time or a long time.

It is impossible to prevent most of the world from being subject to violence, injustice, poverty, and disorder for at least several more generations. But we believe that a process is well started that will make most of the world peaceful, democratic, and wealthy by historical standards by about a century from now, or perhaps two.

Since human society has been dominated by poverty, tyranny, and war for thousands of years, it is easy to argue that our vision of the spread of wealth, democracy, and peace in "only" another century or so is too optimistic. (And we are not at all free from doubt about it.) But since people's lives are shorter than a century, our view of the world also says that billions of human beings are doomed to have their lives cut short or mutiliated by poverty, tyranny and violence. Some may see this view as pessimistic because a century is such a long time.[6]

If Singer and Wildavsky are correct in their views, it would assuredly challenge my own much less sanguine assessment of our prospects. But even such an outcome would not affect the primary aim of this book. This is because its purpose is not to offer yet another prognosis for the future, but rather to reflect on the manner in which humanity generally has looked in that direction; and my purpose in separating Today (which includes some indefinite portion of Tomorrow) from Yesterday is first and foremost to speak of the frame of mind from which our current expectations arise.

Singer and Wildavsky disagree with my assessment of the validity of that change in mood, but they do not deny— indeed, their book is a recognition of—my premise that Today's vision is marked by a new degree of pessimism. From that perspective, their own expectation of a century or more of disruption in the Zones of Violence will quite suffice to support my suggestion that Today's vision differs from Yesterday's. Whether, as they suggest, this is no more than a "fashionable" shift will be a question on which my readers will have to make up their own minds. I will certainly not be sorry if Singer and Wildavsky are right, and Today's vision of the future returns in due course to that of Yesterday. Indeed, as the saying goes, "From their lips to God's ears!" But an exploration of these matters will have to wait until our later pages.

2
THE DISTANT PAST

I

We are already familiar with the future-oriented expectations of the Distant Past. What I want to convey in this chapter is a sense of historical immediacy with regard to that vast period, not only to give substance to what has until now been only an appeal to our intuitive understandings, but because there are lessons to be learned that will have relevance for our condition in the present. But that will have to await some more intimate knowledge of the past than we could have gained from our stratospheric overflight.

It is not surprising that we know nothing whatever about any visions of the future held by our biological ancestors who appeared on earth several million years back, or that our capacity to make plausible guesses about the imagined shape of things to come was still very limited during the early Neanderthal period, only one hundred thousand years ago. Nonetheless, by that time it is a virtual certainty that humankind already anticipated some kind of afterlife. For example, in the Skhul Cave in Israel and the Shanidar Cave in Iraq, skeletons dating back some fifty to sixty thousand years are laid out in fetal positions and provided with food supplies for an implied journey ahead[1]; and in the Archeological Museum in Antalya, Turkey, we can see the 25,000-year-old skeleton of an adult within the remains of a clay pot whose shape was almost certainly meant to represent that of a womb. A few pieces of gold jewelry attest to the social position of the deceased, but the physical position of the corpse—knees drawn up, head down, arms crossed—powerfully suggests that death was seen as rebirth, a climactic event in which the self would change in form and identity but might escape annihilation.

Thus, the idea of the posthumous future as a journey into some other world or life seems strongly indicated as part of the belief system of prehistoric humanity. Its depiction of death as a kind of physical rebirth is naive, but it would be a mistake to regard the idea of life-after-death as merely a primitive notion. All contemplations of the future—magical, religious, social, even scientific—exist at some deep level to deny, or at least to come to terms with, the terrifying prospect of death's finality. The scientific concept of time undoubtedly has attributes that can be described apart from life, but the need to construct the idea of a "future" would be meaningless without the tacit assumption that humanity will be there to inhabit it.

II

The examination of visions of the future as expressions of the ways in which humankind has coped with the concept of death is an Ariadne's thread that will help guide our own vicarious journey through history. Not surprisingly, the thread will be most immediately visible in this first extended "chapter," where we will catch sight of it initially in primitive and magical beliefs concerning an afterlife, later in mythologies of immortality, and later still in elaborate architectures of religious and philosophical belief. But before we begin to probe into these otherworldly imaginings of the future, it is helpful to remind ourselves that the starting point from which our inquiry begins is the state of expectations with respect to the prospects for life on this side of death.

We can begin with a surprising fact. The first ninety-nine percent of human existence is a time in which the species not only survived but flourished. Long before the confident paintings and etchings of the Lascaux and Altamira caves, hunting and gathering societies easily fulfilled the essential task of provisioning themselves. The economist Vernon Smith comments:

Ever since Hobbes there has prevailed the perception that life in the state of nature was 'solitary, poor, nasty, brutish, and short.' A more accurate representation (if not strictly correct in all aboriginal societies) would argue that the hunter culture was the original affluent society. . . . Extensive earlier data on extant hunter-gatherers show that with rare exceptions their food base was at minimum reliable, at best very abundant. The argument that life in the Paleolithic must have been intolerably harsh is simply not borne out by the many ethnographic studies of extant hunting societies in the past century.[2]

A few examples of such hunting and gathering societies have survived into the twentieth century, such as the extensively studied Kalahari bush people and scattered tribes in New Guinea and South America, and it is worth recalling that the "Indians" who inhabited the North

American continent at the time of its English colonization were examples of this most ancient of all social orders.[3] But in an environment that has changed out of all recognition, the general form of tribal social organization is now only a vestigial remnant of its once predominant importance. Hence we are unprepared to learn that anthropological studies generally confirm the view of prehistoric man as a formidable hunter and gatherer—so much a master of his realm, in fact, that a combination of his growing numbers and his fearsome abilities threatened to undermine an abundance posited on a limitless supply of game. In all likelihood, it was the increasing efforts needed to obtain this depleting source of subsistence that played a central role in bringing about a shift from a predominantly hunting-and-gathering mode of production toward slash-and-burn or pastoral modes, and then to settled agriculture.

This last shift does not take place until the last ten thousand years before the first appearance of the great civilizations in the sixth and fifth millennia B.C., but it interests us for a reason that bears directly on our concern with anticipations of the future. For there can be no doubt that a movement into an agricultural mode of life, even if at first only on a tiny village scale, laid the basis for a wholly new increase in the quality and quantity of production. A surplus of grain can be stored for long periods, whereas gatherings of fruit and meat spoil quickly, so that agricultural societies possess the means for supporting a wide range of sustained non-food-related activities, such as threshing, storage, and irrigation, which in turn encourage the development of transportation and building techniques, useless in a nomadic or hunting and gathering social order. To the degree that these new opportunities are seized, they are bound to extend the ability of society to shape and utilize nature, moving outward the general productive capability that economists call the "production possibility frontier." By roughly 8000 B.C., the settlement of Jericho had a population of some two to three thousand and had protected itself with a massive stone wall. Nothing of this kind would have been feasible in the pre-agricultural period.

This increase in material capabilities now raises the larger question of expectations. If a shift to some kind of organized agricultural mode greatly magnifies productive capability—one has only to conjure up the contrast between a Kalahari encampment and the great walled cities and irrigated fields of the Tigris and Euphrates valley—should not the visions of the future entertained by these city-states have risen concomitantly? Would we not expect the poems and sagas of Sumer and Akkad, or of ancient Egypt or all the great early civilizations, to be marked by celebrations of their triumphant rise, and by anticipations for its continuance? Yet such optimistic expressions are not to be found in any of them. On the contrary, writing about the rich civilization of ancient Egypt, the Egyptologist Henri Frankfort describes the emptiness of its views of its future:

[T]he Egyptians had very little sense of history or of past and future. For they conceived their world as essentially static and unchanging. It had gone forth complete from the hands of the Creator. Historical incidents were, consequently, no more than superficial disturbances of the established order, or recurring events of never-changing significance. The past and the future—

23

far from being a matter of concern—were wholly implicit in the present.[4]

Samuel Kramer echoes this finding in reviewing the Sumerian literature of the second and third millennia B.C.:

The Sumerians held out no comforting hopes for man and his future. To be sure, they longed for security and . . . freedom from fear, want, and war. But it never occurred to them to project these longings into the future. Instead, they thought of them in retrospect, and relegated them to the long-gone past[5]

Moreover, the theme continues as new civilizations take the place of older ones. In the eighth century B.C., the Greek poet Hesiod postulated four ages of man—gold, silver, bronze, and iron—each of lesser worth than its predecessor; he deemed his own age to be of iron. Rome celebrated its descent, not its ascent, from Romulus and Remus. Indeed, most mythological history looks back to a never-to-be-equaled past and looks forward to the future with indifference, at best.

III

Given the extraordinary discontinuity between the pre- and posthistoric periods of the Distant Past—I use the appearance of organized states to mark the difference—why did not visions of the future change? One answer of great importance is that the chroniclers of the literate past were utterly unaware of the prehistoric condition of humankind, as indeed was the case until little more than a hundred years ago. The ancients traced their origins—or at least the origins of their rulers—to divine or semidivine ancestors. Egyptian royalty believed itself descended directly from the gods; cultures as different as those of Sumer or Greece or India thought their kings or princes inherited the souls of a remote Heroic Age; and Israelite society looked back to the Garden of Eden.[6] It is not surprising that from such initial assumptions, narratives of history run downward or remain essentially stationary, buffeted by chance but not driven by an underlying current of improvement.

A second answer throws light on the matter by directing our attention to political changes brought about by the shift in the mode of production from a hunting-and-gathering base to settled agriculture. Kinship or tribal societies, it is widely agreed, are egalitarian in their economic arrangements.[7] In its essential form, economic distribution in such a society is based on kinship relations that assure an equitable, although not precisely equal, sharing of the kill or the day's gathering.

This expands our understanding of the static character of the prehistoric past. Society lacked the capability to change its structure in those ways needed to become a posthistoric social order—that is, one in which a new, indisputably higher social order would come into being. An egalitarian socioeconomic order gravitates naturally toward weak institutions of power. The absence of poverty lessens the capability of physically superior individuals to exercise their will over others. The nomadic character of production makes the assertion of property rights impossible, beyond the weapons or household gear of families, diminishing further the possibilities for the domination of a few, however chosen. Kinship rules prevent amassing an undue portion of each day's harvest or kill. Not least, dissatisfied members of one community can leave it to join another or to establish their own clan. Thus, the organized and directed discipline required not merely to build massive buildings, but to institute a massive social structure of command and obedience depended on the very attribute lacking in tribal society— social inequality.

In sharp contrast, settled agricultural societies encourage precisely such social differentiation. Their intimate relationship to a fixed tract of land leads easily to the establishment of boundaries for individual labors of sowing and reaping, so that agriculturally based societies are much more likely than nomadic ones to formalize and recognize personal ownership of land. This by no means implies that all agricultural societies move rapidly toward class differences based on ownership or to the discipline imposed by unequal access to arable land. Indeed, as late as the eighteenth century in Russia, the village council regularly redistributed the lands "belonging" to each family.[8] Nevertheless, as the mode of production moves in the direction of settled cultivation, a "political possibility frontier" shifts outward along with the production possibility frontier. The organizational potential of an agricultural mode of production may not necessitate, but it makes possible a degree of centralization and concentration of social control beyond reach in pre-agricultural societies.

By the fourth and third millennia B.C., the crucial element seems to have been the appearance of what Karl Wittfogel has called "hydraulic agriculture"—systems of centrally controlled water supply that gave vast power to whatever authorities controlled them.[9] The most spec-

tacularly successful of these breakthroughs were the Mesopotamian city-states located on the Tigris and Euphrates
rivers, the Egyptian kingdom of the Nile Valley, the Indus
Valley city-state of Mohenjodaro, and the Shang confedera-
tion along the Yellow River in northern China, all of which
practiced hydraulic agriculture, artificially irrigating their
valley land with flood water. The sociologist-historian
Michael Mann adds a new and very useful consideration—
namely, the ability of such organized communities to
arouse, and in time to demand, an allegiance among families
or groups to their particular "societies," an allegiance that
is absent when borders and boundaries are less clearly de-
finable.

In his view, civilization therefore arises first in communities whose situational characteristics lend themselves to
the "caging" of their individual members, and perhaps of
even greater importance, of the economic, social, ideological, and military organizations by which the larger societal
entity is defined and defended. As such, posthistoric society
is best conceived not as a freely undertaken movement upward, but as a forced adaptation to the boundaries of organized collective life.[10]

IV

These considerations shed more light on why expectations
failed to respond to the extraordinary change between pre-
and posthistoric production capabilities. The reason is that
the enhanced powers of production and social coordination
were not used to ameliorate the conditions of life of the great

27

majority, and more likely caused their relative deterioration. As the anthropologist Marshall Sahlins puts it, "The members of primitive societies have few possessions, but *they are not poor*. Poverty is not a certain small amount of goods, nor is it just a relationship between means and ends; above all it is a relation between people. Poverty is a social status. As such it is the invention of civilization."[11]

There can be no doubt that poverty appears simultaneously with the great civilizations. There is a consensus among historians that wealth was tightly concentrated at the top of the great kingdoms and empires that arose from their alluvial beginnings, and that poverty was widespread and grinding at the bottom. Herodotus, for example, tells us that building just the track along which the stones for the great pyramid of Cheops were to be hauled took the labor of a hundred thousand men for ten years, but he does not record any comparable efforts to improve the lot of the great majority of Cheops's subjects.[12] Nor do we find in later civilizations, such as the Greek or Roman or Ottoman empires, any attempts to spread the visibly growing wealth of their economies among the lower orders, except for doles intended to prevent unrest among the underclass, and spectacles and public entertainments openly acknowledged as opiates for the masses. Reviewing the evidence for Rome, mainly during the first two centuries of the Christian era, the classical historian Ramsey MacMullens writes:

[W]e have at the top of Roman society a quite minute but extraordinarily prominent and rich nobility . . . ; at the bottom, a large mass of the totally indigent, mostly free but partly slave; and strung out between the extremes a variety too heterogeneous to be called in any sense a middle class. . . . The chief purpose of the survey is to suggest what the proportions of the social scale must have felt like. "Verticality" is key to the understanding of it. Great were the differences between the extremes, attenuated the middle parts. The sense of high and low pressed heavily on the consciousness of both.[13]

Hence, as Sahlins suggests, the paradoxical consequence of the advent of civilization was to introduce into society a new social condition of poverty. Moreover, the newborn poverty not only consisted of the relative deprivation that seems to be largely absent from primitive society, but reflected a condition of "absolute" want, arising from the exclusion of a quarter to a third of the population from direct access to the means of subsistence. In part, this exclusion was the consequence of the increase in slave labor that flowed in as the spoils of victorious military campaigns; in part it also reflected the appearance of an internal proletariat, as unlucky or inept individuals lost their lands and thereafter were able to survive only by becoming servants or workers. To stress the point again, no such destitution was possible in a primitive society.

Do these social changes help explain the absence of optimistic expectations regarding the material future? That is a more difficult matter to decide. There is ample testimony that the presence of a restive underclass troubled all the high civilizations during and after the last millennium before Christ, insofar as it weakened the capacity for defense against foreign invasion or domestic unrest. In the case of Rome, for example, the decay of empire was the great focus of Roman disquiet, and here the polarization of wealth and poverty undoubtedly played a role: "The existence of two castes," writes the historian Michael Rostovtzeff, "one ever more oppressed, the other ever more idle and indulging in the easy life of men of means, lay like an incubus on the Empire and arrested economic progress . . . The imperial power rested on privileged classes, and the privileged classes were bound in a very short time to sink into sloth."[14]

Thus, it is tempting to ascribe the gloomy tone of ancient history to the inequities and inefficiencies of its stratified social orders. But we must beware of applying modern-day judgments to times that viewed inequality as a natural aspect of the order of things. "That some should rule and others be ruled is a thing, not only necessary, but expedient," Aristotle wrote in a famous passage; "[F]rom the hour of their birth, some are marked out for subjection, some for rule."[15] In this summary judgment, delivered with the calm force of certitude, we find further evidence of an attitude that bears heavily against any conception of a future that would break decisively with the past. In both the pre- and posthistoric periods of antiquity, the shape of things to come expresses the belief that the future is ultimately beyond human control. In the prehistoric portion of this chapter, the belief derives from the recognition of Nature as a powerful force, against whose rulings there is no appeal. In the much shorter posthistoric portion, Nature begins to yield a considerable degree of its power to the rising productive capacities of stratified societies, but a third—and unchallengeable—element enters the scene: human nature, above all, in the form of the presumed inevitability of a society of great inequality.

Such a view imparts to the future of society the same unyielding fixity as that imparted by Nature in an earlier time. A thousand years after Aristotle we find the same judgment, leading to the same conclusion: Machiavelli writes, "[W]hoever wishes to foresee the future must consult the past; for human events ever resemble those of preceding times. This arises from the fact that they are produced by men who ever have been, and ever will be, animated by the same passions, and thus they necessarily have the same result."[16] An optimistic attitude toward the future is difficult to reconcile with this most profoundly conservative of all ideas.

V

We will return to the question of human nature more than once before we have finished our conspectus of visions of the future, but there remains an aspect of those visions whose importance we have noted, but have not yet described. This is the expectation of existence after death. Here we begin with a return to the prehistoric period, with its mixture of startlingly realistic cave paintings, occasional stylized human figures and "abstract" signs, sculptured figurines, and elaborate burial preparations. There is no definitive interpretation of the meaning of these powerful images, but in an influential article, the sociologist Robert Bellah has suggested a compelling "reading" of their religious import:

Primitive religions are on the whole oriented to a single cosmos— they know nothing of a wholly different world relative to which the actual world is utterly devoid of value. They are concerned with the maintenance of personal, social and cosmic harmony and with attaining specific goods—rain, harvest, children, health—as men have always been. But the overriding goal of salvation that dominates the world-rejecting religions is almost absent in primitive religion, and life after death tends to be a shady semi-existence in some vaguely designated place in the single world.[17]

It is not surprising, therefore, that primitive religious life is characterized by participation, rather than by worship or sacrifice. "In the ritual," Bellah writes, "the participants become identified with the mythical beings they represent. The mythical beings are not addressed or propitiated or beseeched. The distance between man and mythical being, which was at best slight, disappears altogether in the moment of ritual when everything becomes now. There are no priests and no congregation, no mediating representatives and no spectators. All present are involved in the ritual action itself and have become one with the myth."[18]

This reconstruction of preliterate religious life describes from yet another vantage point the characteristic prehistoric projection into the future of the conditions of the present. Nothing in the relics of vanished kinship or tribal societies, or in the testimony gathered from their present descendants implies the expectation of, or the wish for, another kind of life after death. One might think, for instance, that expectations of the future would be enriched by the impending union of those now alive with the spirits that dwell in that realm. But this mingling of self and spirit already exists within the present. The future can therefore only be supposed to continue the present, different in detail but not in overall design. In a manner of speaking, there is neither future nor past in prehistoric societies. There is only an immense present, stretching backward and forward like an ever-changing but always unchanged veld, jungle, ocean, sky.

How can we now describe the corresponding religious vision of posthistoric, literate society? Following Bellah's account, the initial "primitive" stage of religion is followed by an "archaic" phase in which its participatory character gives way to an obsession with propitiation and sacrifice, the currying of favor with one set of gods, and the erection of defenses against the mischievous intervention of others. With this comes a new attitude toward death, nowhere sounded more poignantly than in Greek philosophy. In the *Phaedo,* Plato portrays Socrates describing the "other world" to his friends. He speaks of two prospects. One concerns "those who have been preeminent for holiness of life." "Released from this earthly prison," he declares, "[they] go to their pure home which is above, and dwell in the purer earth; and of these, such as have duly purified themselves with philosophy live henceforth altogether without the body, in mansions fairer still, which may not be described. . . ."

But Socrates has previously made it clear that this is not a destination to be taken for granted. He has spoken of the chasm called Tartarus into whose sulphurous depths are consigned forever those who have committed "many and terrible deeds of sacrilege, [and] murders foul and violent." Even those who have committed less dreadful crimes are also plunged into Tartarus for a year, after which they are cast forth to find their way to the Acherusian Lake, whence they lift up their voices to plead with their victims for mercy.[19]

Socrates accepts the hemlock with a composure that

suggests he knows which of the destinations will be his, but this terrifying vision of the afterlife must be contrasted with the much less unnerving expectations of primitive religious views. And the increased tension of archaic religion is now succeeded by the still more anxiety-laden content of what Bellah calls the "historic" period of religion, whose most important representative in the West is the Christian era. In this period, for the first time, the religious outlook is strongly marked by a transcendental character. "The cosmological monism of the earlier stage is now more or less completely broken through," Bellah writes, "and an entirely different realm of universal reality, having for religious man the highest value, is proclaimed."[20]

. . . For the masses, at least, [he continues] the new dualism is above all expressed in the difference between this world and the life after death. Religious concern, focused on this life in primitive and archaic religions, now tends to focus on life in the other realm, which may be either infinitely superior or, under certain circumstances, with the emergence of various conceptions of hell, infinitely worse. Under these circumstances the religious goal of salvation (or enlightenment, release, and so forth) is for the first time the central religious preoccupation . . . [Transcendental] religions promise man for the first time that he can understand the fundamental structure of reality and through salvation paticipate actively in it. *The opportunity is greater than before but so is the risk of failure.*[21]

What we have here is not only an analysis that sheds light on the evolution of religious ceremony, but one that adds another source of understanding for the unchanging vision of the material future that continues from the prehistoric through the posthistoric eras. Primitive communicants

34

must have known awe and unease in contemplating the afterlife, but they could not have known the kind of terror of which Socrates speaks, for they could not contemplate outcomes that were completely at variance with their participatory acceptance of a spirit-world co-existing—even intermingling—with the real world. Such an acceptance reinforces a passive acquiescence in an unknowable but already familiar future to which their material conditions of life lent immediate support.

Archaic worshippers, on the other hand, already beginning to brave nature with long voyages—one thinks of the Norsemen crossing the Atlantic—could not have known the agony of a refusal of salvation because no such concept existed in their religious universe, but they knew the fear that comes from an inadequate display of piety, or from offenses to gods of whom they were perhaps unaware, or from an improper performance of ritual. Archaic religion thus introduces a cautionary wariness with regard to any future prospects that their improved material life might have suggested—in addition to which, the prospects themselves were intensely personal, not related to possiblities for all.

Finally, in the "historic" form of religion, a new attitude toward the future emerges in the guilt of the individual who is responsible for his or her salvation, and must accept the penalty of a denial of that inestimable reward because of a failure of belief. This gives us insight into the absence of optimistic expectations with respect to life on this earth, even in the last, most materially advanced period of post-historic civilization. Here the absence arises from what Bellah describes as an "extremely negative evaluation of man and society"[22] in all societies in which religion has assumed its "historic" form, with its characteristic risk of spiritual failure. The risk takes on different aspects and delivers different punishments in different cultures, but conveys the same message to all: life is a burden that must be borne, not celebrated—a burden shed only after death, and by no means with certainty even then.

This is, in fact, a message we find in all salvationist societies, poor as well as rich: in the New Testament, in the Buddhist conception of the world as a great burning house from which one must find escape, in Chinese Taoism with its withdrawal from human society, and in Islam, where the Koran compares the world to the vegetation that bursts forth after rain, only to wither away like straw. An existential anxiety is thereby wedded to the concept of life in religious higher civilizations, as a transcendental faith offers both new hope and, as Bellah says, "a far greater degree of risk."

It would be too much to say that Ariadne's thread—visions of the future as a means of coping with the idea of death—suffices to explain the persisting changelessness of material expectations throughout the turns and twists of the Distant Past. At best, successive forms of religion introduce appraisals of the future that reinforce the passive acquiescence that is the great lesson of material and social life. Nonetheless, these religious reinforcements add an appreciation of what must be altered if this view of the future is ever to change. Only some new source of vitalizing energy, manifesting itself as powerfully as a force of nature and possessing something of the authority of religion, can overcome the weightiness and sobriety of all future-oriented conceptions throughout the Distant Past. As I said earlier, no such transformative energy was available throughout the Distant Past because the social dynamics needed to instill it had not yet come into being. This gives us some appreciation of the magnitude of change that will emerge in the period we call Yesterday. As for the relevance of that change for our own times—and perhaps the relevance of the views of the Distant Past, as well—we will have to wait a bit longer.

3
YESTERDAY

I

Yesterday signifies the onset of what we all recognize as "modern" times, a period for which my initial date of c. 1750 is of necessity arbitrary. In many ways the changes that so decisively separate Yesterday from all that has gone before do not make their presence felt until well into the nineteenth century; and looking in the opposite direction, one can easily enough argue that its origins lie much earlier, in the contributions of Newton or, before him, Galileo.

But if the dating of the period is open to question, its identifying characteristic is not. As we know, it is the appearance of forces capable of imparting a new momentum—and with that, a previously unknown horizon of expectations—to the social world. I emphasize "new" momentum, for we must not forget that the Distant Past followed its own course because it also obeyed an immensely powerful force in the inertia of its particular structure, reinforced, as we have seen, by the teachings of various religious systems with respect to the posthumous future. Merely to give substance to this generalization, let us remember that during the disintegration of the Roman Empire—"the greatest, per-

haps, and most awful scene in the history of mankind,''
according to Gibbon—this inertial force retained its conservative influence. Even as a crazy quilt of microfeudalities
replaced the provinces of the Empire, and still later during
the period when that crazy quilt gradually coalesced into a
map of nation-states, the scaffolding of social life remained
much the same: the tasks performed by peasants and workmen; the gulf between the ways of the high and mighty, and
the low and obscure; the lubrication provided by merchants
for the workings of the socioeconomic whole—all these
were in some large sense the same throughout three millennia of Egyptian history, seven centuries of Roman rule, and
a thousand years of medieval life.

This persisting stability provides the necessary base
against which to measure the achievement that would now
alter the social landscape almost as dramatically as did the
ascent of the escarpment from the prehistoric to the posthistoric periods of the Distant Past. Moreover, the changes
that now emerge are not once-and-for-all, but continuous,
so that the social structure is never again stationary, its tasks
constantly altering, the relation of top and bottom always
under pressure, and the lubricating function of commerce
rapidly transforming into a torrent that cuts riverbeds
through the economic landscape. As a result, in only two
hundred years, Yesterday gives birth to alterations nearly as
far-reaching as those that required at least two thousand
years during the only period in the Distant Past that bears
comparison in terms of its transformative properties.

One last preliminary remark is needed. Not only is
Yesterday marked by a degree of dynamism for which no
parallel exists earlier, but it also endorses and explains this

dynamic tendency in a two-syllable word for which there is no equivalent, either in primitive or stratified society. The word is "progress," a term with many specific meanings, but one overarching signification: that the present is in some fashion superior to the past and, by extension, that the future will be superior to the present. The most moving expression of that belief may well have come from the philosopher Condorcet, who wrote (before taking his life to avoid the guillotine) that "[H]uman perfectibility is in reality infinite, [and] the progress of this perfectibility, henceforth independent of any power that might wish to stop it, has no other limit than the duration of the globe upon which nature has placed us," to which he added, no doubt referring to his own situation:

What a picture of the human race, freed from its chains, removed from the empire of chance as from that of the enemies of its progress, and advancing with a firm and sure step on the pathway of truth, of virtue, and of happiness, is presented to the philosopher to console him for the errors, the crimes, and the injustices with which the earth is still soiled, and of which he is often the victim![1]

Our task is accordingly laid out for us. We must identify the nature of the revolutionary transformations that will become the historic forces of this period, and examine the manner in which these transformations establish a radically new vision of the shape of things to come. We should bear in mind, however, that although this vision is still very much with us as a perspective on the future, it is also, if I am right, one that is now in the process of change.

II

The control over nature seems the proper starting place for this inquiry, insofar as it is obviously an essential prerequisite for the idea of progress. Yet this control does not enter our chapter as a new force within history for the reason we might think—namely, because it is given an extraordinary leverage by the development of science. On the contrary, the mastery of fire; the techniques of shaping flint and bone into tools for cutting, scraping, sewing, drilling, and hunting; the improvement of the means of transportation from hand-drawn sleds to animal-drawn barrows and wagons; the development of agriculture and irrigation; the building of shelters; the spinning of thread and weaving of cloth; and the hewing of stone are all momentous advances in productive capability that emerged not from any abstract inquiry, but from innumerable individual departures and discoveries, no doubt often opposed in the name of tradition and custom. Taken individually, these improvements could not have exerted a perceptible effect on the production frontier, but collectively they were sufficient to lay the basis for the mastery of the alluvial agriculture that in turn made possible the climb to organized civilization.

Indeed, by the third millennium B.C., prescientific technology had yielded the ability to cut and transport the massive blocks of the pyramids; by the third century B.C., to build the magnificent lighthouse that towered above the harbor entrance to Alexandria—the tallest lighthouse that has ever been constructed—and by the second century A.D., to create a system of water supply in Rome (including hot water for many houses), together with sewage and garbage disposal and public amenities that would remain basically unsurpassed until modern times.

Why, then, was technology not already a recognized force with respect to visions of the future long before the eighteenth century? As we have already noted, the reason was not the absence of a core of pre-scientific knowledge beneath this impressive, although slow and irregular, advance in technology. All cooperation with nature requires, and gives rise to, a body of tried-and-true practices that serves as a powerful guide to action long before it has been distilled into systematized science. This gradually accumulating body of "lore" is part of what the economic historian Joel Mokyr calls the "meta-technological knowledge from which technology [draws] its inspiration, consciously or subconsciously."[2] Another part is magic. As Sir James Frazer pointed out in *The Golden Bough,* in primitive society "[Magic] assumes that in nature one event follows another necessarily and invariably without the intervention of any spiritual or personal agency. Thus, its fundamental conception is identical to that of modern science; underlying the whole system is a faith, implicit but real and firm, in the order and uniformity of nature."[3]

As a result, technology can develop without formal science, in the modern sense of a systematized inquiry into the properties of "nature." The absence of a scientific ethos did not prevent the Chinese from producing cast iron fifteen hundred years, and the modern horse collar one thousand years, before the West; from far exceeding Europe in the accuracy of its clocks; or from inventing and using paper for books and money (as well as for lavatory purposes) while Europeans were using parchment, coins, and unsanitary sponges.[4]

More to the point, the belated Western technological overtaking of China in the nineteenth century was not the direct fruit of Newton's or Boyle's scientific discoveries. It was mainly the product of inspired amateur inventors such as James Watt, the designer of the steam engine; of dedicated manufacturers such as John Wilkinson, the ironmaker; and of hard-working scoundrels like the barber Samuel Arkwright who embezzled the design of the spinning jenny from which England gained much of the impetus of the first industrial revolution. Even the so-called second industrial revolution at the end of the last century, although directly science-dependent for the development of its new chemical industry, continued to rely mainly on pre-scientific technologies and techniques for the advances in automobiles and petroleum that provided its principal momentum.

What was it, then, that imparted such a galvanizing impetus to the activities of production during the period we call Yesterday? One explanation is that the kind of abstract knowledge characteristic of scientific investigation gradually becomes conjoined with the lore of practical technology. Although scientists played virtually no direct role in the development of the steam, coal, and textile technologies of the opening decades of the century, their work was at the very heart of the ever-more-important electrical technology of its last decades; and of course would be the sine qua non for the omnipresent computers and looming nuclear silos of the century to come. Thus the "lever of riches" has slowly but steadily increased its power as technology has turned to science for its fulcrum.

A second explanation for the elevation of the prestige of science bears more directly on the change in expectations that is the theme of this chapter. Here the crucial element is the growing enthusiasm for the marvels with which science was associated in the public mind, whether or not at the factory site. Samuel Smiles, a crusading enthusiast for the new technology, wrote in 1857 that "[to] witness a railway train, some five-and-twenty years ago, was an event in one's life." The economic historian Michael Adas tells us more:

No invention rivaled the railroad in capturing the imagination of poets, novelists, and social commentators. William Thackeray suggested that railway tracks provided the "great demarcation line between past and present," while Tennyson exclaimed, after viewing a passing train, "Let the great world spin on forever down the ringing grooves of change." But words do not convey the Victorian's exhilaration at the power of the railroad as wonderfully as J. M. W. Turner's *Rain, Steam, and Speed,* which was painted in 1844 at the height of the British railway mania. The locomotive racing unimpeded through a swirling storm proclaims that the Europeans have devised a machine that allows them to challenge the elements themselves.[5]

Meanwhile, behind the exhilaration of the locomotive, there was the even more remarkable, although less romanticized, transformation wrought by the stationary steam engine. We get some impression of its magnitude when we realize that in Adam Smith's day, the twenty to thirty manufactories in England depended heavily on water-driven power and the muscular effort of six thousand to twelve thousand men, women, and children. A century later, a vastly expanded British industry would have required the labor of forty million workers—more than the population of the country—had it depended on the technology of Smith's time. In fact, the new level of output was made possible by the labor of only four hundred thousand miners in the pits, who produced the coal that fueled the steam engines that drove British factories.[6] Looking back over this increasingly fecund union of science and technology, William H. McNeill has written that the fundamental revolution of mind and spirit took at least two centuries to come to completion, but that in the end, "scientific progress . . . prepared the way for the deliberate and conscious linkage between science and technology which constitutes what is probably the most important contemporary spring of social change."[7]

There is one last consideration before we proceed. Science rises to a position of extraordinary importance because it now begins to supplant religion, the central visionary element of the past. In his influential *The Condition of Man,* written as the chapter of Yesterday was drawing to a close, Lewis Mumford describes the immense moral authority that devolved upon the pursuit of science during the period under our examination—an authority at once different from, and yet reminiscent of, religion. Unlike religion, science did not invoke the name of God to explain the nature of things, but like religion it sought to reveal a hidden design behind its apparent accidental order. Unlike religion, science did not seek its deepest insights in a kind of transcendental rapture, but like religion it insisted on a kind of monastic purity and discipline as it carried out its researches. Not least, just as religion built its moral strength on the overlapping and con-

48

sistent testimony of its great figures, so science, too, gained its stature from an immense interconnected testimony that gradually endowed its collective undertaking with something of a Church-like infallibility—not in any individual instance, but as a mode of inquiry, a source of understanding.

Finally, like religion, science was interested in foreseeing the future, but unlike religion, it turned to observation, not inspiration. As Mumford notes, already in the seventeenth century, Halley's successful prediction of the appearance of the comet that now bears his name was a harbinger of the passage of the miraculous "from the unpredictable to the predictable," which is to say, from the realm of the supernatural to that of the student of nature itself.[8]

III

Needless to say, we have by no means finished with the role of science as it affects the shape of things to come, but while we are still tracing the advent of Yesterday, we must look at another vision-shaping force, separate from but closely intertwined with technology and science. It is the emergence of a new social order, for which the name "capitalism" would not be coined until the late nineteenth century. To describe the processes by which feudal society gave birth to its wholly unintended successor would require a volume far more extensive than this. But there is a shortcut that will bring us quickly to the change in expectations that went along with this lengthy and complex process. It is to move from science, broadly interpreted, to capitalism, via the stepping stone of economics. By economics I mean a form of inquiry absent from the Distant Past—namely, an attempt to understand the manner in which societies handle their own material provisioning, similar to the manner in which men had long sought to understand the revolutions of the planets, the phases of the moon, and the eclipses of the sun.

It is not surprising that the Distant Past had no interest in mounting such an inquiry, for until the eighteenth century, the process of material provisioning was largely under the guidance of tradition or command, neither of which posed what we would call "economic" problems. Tradition was concerned only with maintaining long-established practices and relationships that assured the replenishment of society's needs, a state of affairs that certainly did not suggest the presence of questions requiring a special mode of investigation. Command, of course, raised many problems—we can imagine the disruptions caused by the necessity to recruit and feed the army of laborers who built the pyramids—but even here the problems were those of political authority and technical engineering, not of the kind that we would call "economic."

Economics begins to show its hand only when the mechanisms of tradition and command give way to a new arrangement in which production and distribution come under the charge of three institutions that had previously existed only in embryo or on the fringes of society. One of these was the ever-widening presence of unregulated markets as the means of determining what would be produced and on what terms it would be made available. A second was the appearance of a powerful drive for the accumulation of capital as the central preoccupation, even passion, of a mercantile capitalist class, a stratum whose importance was steadily moving from the fringes of society to its center. And the third was the appearance of a new social realm—a "private" domain of money-making activity, from which government was increasingly excluded by law as well as practice. Government still waged war and conducted diplomacy, was responsible for internal peace and order, and served as the ceremonial center of society, but it was more and more separated from the activities of production and distribution that underpinned the whole. As a consequence, the role of the merchant-capitalist class steadily grew in importance, although its political status remained carefully subordinated to that of the aristocracy.

Economics now takes on the characteristics of a "science"—although it would not be called that until much later—concerned with understanding and explaining the consequences of this previously unknown, seemingly anarchic state of affairs. In an *Essay on the Nature of Commerce* written in the 1730s, Richard Cantillon, an English financial speculator residing in France, caught a clear view of one of its problems, as well as a glimmer of its resolution. In this passage he is trying to understand how the market works:

Suppose [he writes] the Butchers on one side and the Buyers on the other. The price of Meat will be settled after some altercations. . . . The Butcher keeps up his Price according to the number of Buyers he sees; the Buyers, on their side, offer less according as they think the Butcher will have less sale: the Price set by some is usually followed by others. Some are more clever in puffing up their wares, other[s] in running them down. Though this method of fixing Market prices has no exact or geometrical foundation . . . it does not seem that it could be done in any more convenient way. It is clear that the quantity of Produce or of Merchandise offered for sale, in proportion to the demand or number of Buyers, is the basis on which is fixed or always supposed to be fixed the actual Market Prices; and that in general these prices do not vary much from the intrinsic value.[9]

Cantillon, it is clear, is on the verge of formulating a "scientific" explication of a social process—that is, an explanation that finds invisible regularities where there seems to be only chaos. The conception, in which "laws" of supply and demand play roles not too different from those of Newtonian gravity, would not appear in full dress until 1776, when Adam Smith published *The Wealth of Nations,* and its geometrical representation—familiar to every economics student today as the criss-cross of supply and demand curves—would not enter the general discourse for another century.

For all its inexactitude, Cantillon's analysis nonetheless puts its finger on a wholly new understanding—namely, that competitively determined market prices, notwithstanding the puffery and shrewdness of sellers and buyers, approximate the "intrinsic" value of things. From this it is only a short step to seeing that a market system must somehow give rise to order-bestowing processes that had not existed in the past. Hence, the first objective of the new inquiry was to explain how these market forces would bring the prices and production of goods and services into line with their normal costs and with the demand for them at different prices. One of the major contributions of *The Wealth of Nations* was to make clear how a congeries of such markets would constitute a "system" that would assure the material well-being of the public, provided that government did not interfere unduly with its "altercations."

The discovery of an orderliness brought about by the free play of market activity provided a first glimpse of new forces at work within a still-emerging capitalism. There was, however, another, even more powerful force that Cantillon only glimpsed out of the corner of his eye, and that even Smith did not fully appreciate. It was the seismic pressure exerted by the accumulation of capital. We have noted in passing the precondition for this change in the cleavage of a formerly seamless socioeconomic order into two realms: one public, one private. Under this condition, a vital change takes place in the drive for wealth. In what we may now call precapitalist societies, wealth on a major scale was almost exclusively gained through military prowess or strategic political position, not through the always slightly disreputable channels of trade. In the emerging capitalist order, however, the accumulation of wealth through trade or production becomes more and more the means by which the rising mercantile class—unlikely to seek military fame, and unwelcome in the ranks of political preferment—satisfies its own desire for power and prestige. As such, the drive for capital displays the same apparently illimitable hunger as we see in the precapitalist ambitions of kings and emperors.

There is, however, a difference of great importance. Harnessed to the institutions of a capitalist system, wealth itself changes from a testimony to power or prestige of other kinds, mainly military or political, to a representation of power and prestige deriving directly from a process of continuous buying-and-selling. In this sequence, money buys commodities of any sort—iron ore is as good as uncut diamonds—which are combined with labor to create more valuable commodities—ingots or polished gems—that will then be sold at a profit in order to set the process into motion again and again. In early capitalism, this self-expansive process was often realized through family dynasties, the second generation seeking to enlarge the capital of the first, the third or fourth generations retiring to a life of leisure. As the system became increasingly institutionalized, family firms gave way to managerial, then corporatized enterprises engaged in a pursuit of boundless extent.

A great deal of moral criticism has been directed at this ceaseless quest for wealth as the institutionalization of greed, and at least as much approval has been voiced on behalf of its energy-mobilizing consequences. It is the latter that interests us more at the moment, as we look into the manner in which the pursuit of capital becomes a history-shaping force. For the ubiquitous effort to accumulate capital introduces a tremendous economic pressure that spreads throughout the system. From this pressure comes a previously absent source of encouragement to technology, and later to its handmaiden science, as each firm seeks to improve or change its product in a never-ending search for a larger market share.

In this way, capitalism becomes, by nature of its structure and its motivation, the source of the dynamism that was quickly to be the envy and despair of the noncapitalist world. In the *Communist Manifesto,* published in 1848, Marx and Engels have written the least likely, and therefore the most impressive, statement of the case:

The bourgeoisie, during its rule of scarce one hundred years, has created more massive and more colossal productive forces than have all preceding generations together. Subjection of nature's forces to man, machinery, application of chemistry to industry and agriculture, steam-navigation, railways, electric telegraphs, clearing of whole continents for cultivation, canalization of rivers, whole populations conjured out of the ground—what earlier century had even a presentiment that such productive forces slumbered in the lap of social labour?[10]

This is not yet, however, a full account of the effects exerted by the expansive pressure on the social order. Having acknowledged its positive contribution in eloquent words, Marx and Engels go on to qualify the effects of accumulation in words equally as powerful but much more troubling:

Modern bourgeois society with its relations of production, of exchange and of property, a society that has conjured up such gigantic means of production and exchange, is like the sorcerer who is no longer able to control the powers of the nether world whom he has called up by his spells. . . . It is enough to mention the commercial crises that by their periodical return put the existence of the entire bourgeois society on its trial, each time more threateningly. . . . In these crises there breaks out an epidemic that, in all earlier epochs, would have seemed an absurdity—the epidemic of over-production. Society suddenly finds itelf back into a state of momentary barbarism; it appears as if a famine, a universal war of devastation had cut off the supply of every means of subsistence; industry and commerce seem to be destroyed. And why? Because there is too much civilization, too much means of subsistence, too much industry, too much commerce[11]

Marx and Engels were not alone in recognizing the two-edged effect of the capitalist order. Three-quarters of a century before *The Manifesto,* Adam Smith clearly understood the expansive property of the system taking form under his eyes and also its destructive effects. It is the latter insight that surprises us. Smith fails to perceive capital expansion in the dynamic and dramatic terms of Marx's industrial scenario, but that does not lead him to think that the wealth of the nation will therefore increase without end. On the contrary, it will come to a stop once a country acquires "the full complement of riches" for which it has use. After that, the long ascent will turn into a long decline.[12]

From Marx's point of view, with its emphasis on continuous industrial change, Smith's words are naive, but when we look to a second cause for disquiet, it is Marx who seems the less perceptive of the two. Here they are both considering the effect of the numbing routines of capitalist production on the mental and moral condition of the worker. For Marx, the effect is eventually to instill a steely resolve and a political clarity into the minds of the labor force, preparing it for the decisive role it will play in the revolutionary passage beyond capitalism into socialism. Smith has a different view. He foresees the division of labor as grinding down the moral as well as the intellectual capabilities of those exposed to its effects, until—in words that take us by surprise:

[the laborer] generally becomes as stupid and ignorant as it is possible for a human creature to become. The torpor of his mind renders him, not only incapable of relishing or bearing a part in any rational conversation, but of conceiving any generous, noble, or tender sentiment, and consequently of forming any just judgment concerning many even of the ordinary duties of private life. Of the great and extensive interests of his country he is altogether

incapable of judging. . . . [I]n every improved and civilized society this is the state into which the labouring poor, that is, the
great body of the people, must necessarily fall, unless government
takes some pains to prevent it.[13]

This is not to suggest that Marx and Smith are brothers
under the skin, although they are far from being the polar
opposites of popular supposition. Moreover, as we shall see
in our next chapter, neither the sociopolitical nor the economic expectations of either were fully borne out in the
period after the mid-nineteenth century. At this juncture,
however, we should note that very much in accord with the
expectations of both, the immediate consequences of capitalism were to impart to the system a dynamism beyond
anything that had previously been within the scope of imag-
inative, much less actual reach. In the hope of calming the
agitation caused by rising food prices in 1783, the great
potter Josiah Wedgwood wrote *An Address to the Young
Inhabitants of the Pottery,* calling on them "to ask your
parents for a description of the country we inhabit when they
first knew it. . . . Their houses were miserable huts, the
lands poorly cultivated and yielded little of value for the
food of man or beast. . . . Compare this picture, which I
know to be a true one, with the present state of the same
country, the workmen earning near double their former
wages, their houses mostly new and comfortable, and the
land, roads, and every other circumstance bearing evident
marks of the most pleasing and rapid improvement. . . .
Industry has been the parent of this happy change."[14]

Wedgwood's affirmative appraisal owed at least as
much to his own reformist efforts as to economic trends that
were uneven in effect and slow in taking hold. It would be a

hundred years before the wages of an ordinary workman in England would suffice to keep his family adequately housed and fed. Nevertheless, in the end the new order displayed a momentum that was to become its historical hallmark. The economic historian Shepherd Clough has summed up the overall performance of capitalism as follows:

The historian of the mid-twentieth century who studies the economic development of Western culture of the last 150 years is struck at once by the enormous quantitative increase in the production of goods and services. Just how great the increase was is difficult to state in precise terms, but . . . what evidence we have indicates more than a doubling of French national income from 1850 to World War II, a quadrupling of that of Germany for the same period, a tripling of that of Italy from 1860 to 1938, and an eightfold increase in that of the United States from 1869–1878 to 1929–1938. Such increases made possible a rise in the population of Europe from some 187,693,000 people in 1800 to over 530,000,000 in 1938 and in the United States from 4,000,000 in 1790 to 140,000,000 in 1946. Over the entire period there was an increase in income per capita of some two to four times.[15]

IV

There remains a third source of the dynamism that so sharply separates Yesterday from the Distant Past—a source that we have called its "political will." The term refers to the manner in which people accept, celebrate, or seek to alter the relationships of sub- and superordination—the power to command and the necessity to obey—that we find in all postprimitive societies. This returns us, of course, to an aspect of "human nature" of which we have caught sight in the previous chapter—namely, the active embrace in all stratified societies of dominating power above and acquiescence below, once tribalism gives way to "caged" societies.

Surprisingly little attention has been paid to the root sources of this relationship of social hierarchy, in itself a commentary with regard to the phenomenon on which we seek to shed some light. It is sometimes held that all such arrangements are maintained by force, whether overtly displayed or allowed to lurk in the background, but if that accounts for relationships of master and slave, it does not seem to apply to the great majority of social orders, in which the lower classes support, not merely accept, arrangements that to an outsider seem patently unfair or exploitative. Nor does the introduction of force as the key to inequality raise a key question as to the sources and nature of the exercise of power itself. As Ernest Becker puts it: "The thing that has to be explained in human relations, is precisely the *fascination of the person* who holds or symbolizes power."[16]

Where shall we look for an elucidation of these matters? Following Freud and Ferenczi, Becker locates the "aura" of power in the infantile surrender to, and dependence on, the power of the parent. Along the same lines, we can trace both the adult desire to dominate and its converse, the appeal of subservience, to the individual circumstances of the universal passage from childhood into adulthood. The rages, fears, and frustrations of infantile dependency are thus the raw material whence arise both the desire to command and the willingness to obey that uphold the differentiations of castes, classes, priesthoods, and kings, not to mention property. We experience both its infantile nature and its powerful appeal when we feel a "thrill" from catching a glimpse of a billionaire, or lose ourselves in the celebration of a hero.

I do not mean that the recognition of political will as a force for change reflected any intimations of these unconscious roots of political behavior—such an awareness would not appear until its closing decades. I mean the much more naive, but perhaps for that very reason much more stirring, appearance of a new belief in the inherent virtue and dignity of the lower classes. As Kant put it, in endorsing the French Revolution as the essential expression of that will, the event *"cannot be forgotten* because it reveals in human nature a disposition and a capacity for improvement."[17] At the same time, the historian Priscilla Robertson expresses perfectly the "parental" disapproval against which this new idea had to contend. Speaking of the outlook of the upper classes concerning the legitimacy of the political participation of the lesser classes, she writes:

Albert, the workingman, was called by his first name all the time he was a member of the French government; Baron Doblhoff in Vienna was suspected because he gave parties where the nobility could meet the middle classes socially for the first time; the King of Prussia could label an assembly of professors "the gutter"; Macaulay could stand up in the House of Commons to say that universal suffrage would destroy civilization and everything that made civilization worthwhile, the security of property; . . . Metternich doubted that society could exist along with freedom of the press; in Vienna an officer threw his shaving water out the window, and the worker whom he drenched was arrested because he complained; Guizot was shocked that anyone could confound the welfare of the lower classes with that of society as a whole. In such a climate of opinion it is not strange that even those men who had the ideal of democracy in their hearts found it was difficult to explain to others, and almost as hard to live with themselves.[18]

These sentiments were voiced, we should note, in the mid-nineteenth century, in the wake of a repressive anti-democratic wave of political sentiment. Thus, the acceptance of the popular political will did not spread easily as part of the European Enlightenment whose banner was rationalism, not democracy. Nor did the legitimation of the idea of government by the people arise by the instantaneous transplantation into Europe of the American belief in the equality of men, enunciated in the Declaration of Independence that was saluted in Britain even by the conservative Edmund Burke. Rather, the new political spirit entered the European scene as the side effect of the unexpected revolution that exploded in France in 1789, to be immediately attacked by the same Edmund Burke.

In retrospect, at least, it is not surprising that an age which makes progress its motto eventually broadens its interpretation of that term to include the political as well as the intellectual liberation of man. In addition, we can understand how the movement toward political equality takes on a greater urgency in societies that are quickening their pace under the stimulus of deep-reaching socioeconomic change at whose center lay the replacement of involuntary serf labor by contractual wage labor. The term "wage slavery" would soon become a rallying cry for the reformers and revolutionists of nascent capitalism, but it is easy to forget that the oppressions of wage slavery can, in principle, be walked away from, whereas those of serfdom cannot.

The legitimation of political will was thus a gradual and

uneven process. In France, it had begun even before the Revolution as the grudging admission of the well-to-do bourgeoisie into the affairs of state; thereafter, in England, toward the end of the eighteenth century, in the cautious enfranchisement of the propertied middle class—even the prosperous Adam Smith did not possess the financial qualifications to entitle him to vote; followed a century later by the admission to the polls of skilled urban artisans but not town or country laborers; and at last, toward the end of the century, by the enfranchisement of all males.

Long-drawn-out, hesitant, and reluctant as it was, the rise of political will, once commenced, could not be stopped. Lynn Hunt has eloquently conveyed the many-sided effect of that irregular but irreversible process:

The chief accomplishment of the French Revolution was the institution of a dramatically new political culture. The Revolution did not startle its contemporaries because it laid the foundations for capitalist development or political modernization. The English found more effective ways to encourage the former, and the Prussians showed that countries could pursue the latter without democracy or revolution. . . . What [the Revolution] did establish, however, was the mobilizing potential of democratic republicanism and the compelling intensity of revolutionary change. The language of national regeneration, the gestures of equality and fraternity, and the rituals of republicanism were not soon forgotten. Democracy, terror, Jacobinism, and the police state all became recurrent features of political life. . . . Once revolutionaries acted on Rousseau's belief that government could form a new people, the West was never again the same.[19]

There was, in addition, another effect: the introduction of the specter that the *Communist Manifesto* of 1848 declared to be haunting Europe. In fact, it was not communism as we have known it, but various ideas of socialism that were the first representatives of a political will that went beyond the demand for a voice in government to the goal of democratizing the system of production itself. In England the earliest such schemes were paternalistic ventures, launched by the reform-minded mill-owner Robert Owen; in France they took on more ambitious, "utopian" forms, of which the most famous were perhaps the *phalansteries* of Charles Fourier—half retirement homes for the nonretired, half kibbutzim—from which sprang dozens of utopian communities in the United States in the second half of the nineteenth century.

The utopian socialist movement earned only the scorn and ridicule of the authors of the *Manifesto*. Had they been less scornful, Marx and Engels might have paid more heed to the *Principles of Political Economy,* also published in 1848, by John Stuart Mill, who would become the dominant figure in English economic thought over the next quarter-century. Mill was not altogether hostile to the institutions of capitalism—"while minds are coarse they require coarse stimuli, and let them have them"[20]—but he believed that working men would not long permit themselves to be kept in "leading strings" by their employers, and after a time would combine to take over their firms, presumably in a mutually agreeable settlement. After that, with Mill's blessing, the existing economic system—still not named "capitalism"— would become a socialism characterized by worker-owned competitive enterprises.

Marx's and Engel's clarion call was a great deal less acceptable than Mill's peaceful evolutionary prospect. The complex mixture of political desanctification and economic analysis that came to be known as Marxism saw the demise of capitalism as a process driven by the self-engendered contradictions of the system and the gradually intensifying political consciousness of the proletariat. The specter was thus one of economic breakdown and political revolution, not of economic slowdown and political evolution.

There is little need to recount the subsequent history of that mixture of "science" and hope, but assuredly Marxism did come to haunt Europe (and America) in a manner that the democratic political will by itself did not. More than fifteen years before the *Manifesto* appeared, Alexis de Tocqueville had written about the rise of democracy in America: "[t]he gradual development of equality of conditions has the principal characteristic of a providential fact. It is universal, it is permanent, it eludes human power; all events and all men serve this development. . . ."[21] The irresistible force attributed by de Toqueville to the drive for political democracy was for a time a specter that haunted some parts of Europe, but one with which European capitalism found it could make an accommodation. The prospect of the drive for democracy directed not at the form of government, but at the system of ownership, was far more frightening, especially after the successful Russian Revolution of 1917. The truly utopian hopes and prospects aroused by that spectacular event were vividly expressed by the brash young American reporter Lincoln Steffens, returning in 1919 from Petrograd: "I have seen the future," he wrote to a friend, "and it works." I dare say that very few of those who were shocked and frightened by such declarations in the heady early years of the revolution recognized in its rhetoric the political will of Yesterday come to full flower.

V

How shall we sum up the visions of the future that arose from the extraordinary changes to which this chapter has been devoted? There is no simple way to combine the awed respect for technology, the recognition of the dynamic properties of capitalism, and the celebration of the long-denied appearance of political will, at least before it took its "subversive" turning. It is not even a simple matter to accord priorities to these three central forces: the events of Yesterday were integrally connected with technological and then scientific advance, which in turn were inextricably intertwined with the momentum of capitalism, which in its own turn was both a powerful source of, and eventually a target for the popular political will.

Moreover, as we shall see in our next chapter, there were doubters and dissenters with respect to all three major forces—questioning voices whose influence grew larger as Yesterday moved toward Today. In 1908, Arthur Balfour, former Prime Minister of England, could declare that "no symptoms either of pause or regression" could be discovered in the "onward movement which for more than a thousand years [had] been characteristic of Western civilization," but in that same year the French syndicalist Georges Sorel published *Les illusions du progrès,* denouncing that key two-syllable word as bourgeois dogma designed to cover over the actual decadence of the times.[22] The last years of the nineteenth century thus became marked with a spirit of *fin de sièclisme* that denigrated or even rejected the advances that science, capitalism, and political will had brought, or presumably would bring.

These themes will come to the fore in our next chapter, but it would be a great error to give them undue prominence in concluding this one. The spirit of the times was not one of doubt. The visible diminution of what Marx called "rural idiocy"; the rise of the commercial excitement of the city; the lengthening of life and assuagement of pain brought by the discovery of anesthetics, vaccines, and a scientific approach to medicine in general; the widening access to education; the explosion of industry despite its recurrent depressions and increasingly disquieting side effects; and the gradual acceptance, even embrace of political democracy all seemed to embody a profound, unique, and irreversible change in the human condition. The historian Bury sums up the seventies and eighties of the last century as a time when "the idea of Progress was becoming a general article of faith. . . . The majority did not inquire too curiously into . . . points of doctrine, but received it in a vague sense as a comfortable addition to their convictions. . . . [I]t became part of the general mental outlook of educated people."[23] The focus that must not be lost to sight is a comparison between that vision and the vision of the Distant Past, when the prevalent belief was that of a descent from some distant Golden Age, or the prospect of a future in which the human condition would be imprisoned in the iron maiden of its own nature. It is this pessimistic reference point that disappears in the period we call Yesterday, to resurface, although in different guise, Today.

4
TODAY

I

Resignation sums up the Distant Past's vision of the
future; hopefulness was that of Yesterday; and apprehension is the dominant mood of Today. I make that appraisal in full awareness that it cannot carry the weight of
near-unanimous agreement that attaches to my assessment
of the preceding two chapters' visions of things to come; but
I make the appraisal nonetheless with a considerable degree
of confidence. Even Aaron Wildavsky and Max Singer,
whose *The New World Order* we briefly examined in the
Preview, acknowledged the "fashionable pessimism" of
the moment, against which they directed the thrust of their
book. Moreover, looking across the main developments of
the last decade or two, it is difficult to imagine any mood
other than apprehension and anxiety that would reflect the
experiences we have lived through: the totally unforeseen
outburst of bloodthirsty violence in what used to be called
Yugoslavia, not so long ago the locus of an optimistic literature of forward-looking democratic socialism; the descent
into desperation of Soviet society, following the dissolution
of its empire; the maelstrom of Central Africa; the rise of

skinheads in Germany and a neo-fascist movement in Italy; and not least the breakdown of civil society at home, both within and, to a lesser extent, outside the boundaries of the inner city. Each of these events, in itself, would have been traumatic; taken together they have hypnotized and horrified the public imagination to a degree unimaginable some forty-odd years ago when we crossed over the invisible divide from Yesterday into Today.

It is important that we begin our examination of Today by stressing its difference from Yesterday, but it is no less important to recognize an attribute that links us indissolubly with the period we have left behind. This is the continued presence of the three forces that were the shaping determinants of Yesterday. The empowering gift of science, the relentless dynamics of a capitalist economy, and the spirit of mass politics still constitute the forces leading us into the future. The difference is that these forces are no longer regarded unambiguously as carriers of progress. Rather, the outlook for the future has turned because negative aspects of those agencies for change—some previously unknown, some seen but largely ignored—are today widely recognized as warranting at least as much, perhaps even more attention than their undisputed positive effects.

This is not to say that we live in an age of despair, or expect the coming of some final judgment, as did the believers who climbed mountaintops in Europe in the year 999. Today's mood is somber rather than black; uncertain rather than despairing; and still strongly dependent on the forward momentum of the triad of forces in our midst, while newly mindful of their dangerous side—or even direct—effects. Thus I must stress as well as repeat that I assess our contemporary frame of mind as ambiguous, indeterminate, and apprehensive—a state of affairs that reflects, as did the mindsets of the past, the nature and developmental logic of the underlying social realities themselves.

II

Let me begin again with science, which, as late as the 1870s, was still regarded as a threat to religion: Darwin's *Descent of Man,* published in 1871, provoked a major theological crisis. Yet, as we have already noted, by the end of the century, science not only had lost its threatening aspect, even to theologians, but was becoming a kind of popular stand-in for religion, one that offered a view of the world both orderly and inspirational.

What was it that undermined—it never entirely undone—that reassuring presence? One powerful cause was the gradual coming into being of misgivings that had in fact been voiced well back into the nineteenth century. Thomas Carlyle, who was certainly not blind to the advances produced by technology, saw in the undue elevation of the importance attached to mechanical processes the ultimate destruction of "Moral Force." "By our skill in Mechanism," he wrote in 1829, "it has come to pass, that in the management of external things we excel all other ages; while in whatever respects the pure moral nature, in true dignity of soul and character, we are perhaps inferior to most civilized ages." The social historian and critic Leo Marx comments that it is but a short step from Carlyle's "destruction of Moral Force" to Karl Marx's term "alienation'' and to his warning in 1844 that '' 'The *devaluation* of the human world increases in direct relation with the *increase in value* of the world of things.' '' Three years later, Emerson takes up the same theme, in words that have become familiar:

> Things are in the saddle,
> And ride mankind.

> There are two laws discrete,
> Not reconciled,—
> Law for man, and law for thing;
> The last builds town and fleet,
> But it runs wild,
> And doth man unking.[1]

Moral and aesthetic murmurs were not, however, the decisive factors in altering the public attitude toward science and technology. That change was unquestionably connected with armed conflict. As the social historian Michael Adas writes with respect to the impact of World War I on public awareness:

The theme of humanity betrayed and consumed by the technology that Europeans had long considered the surest proof of their civilization's superiority runs throughout the accounts of those engaged in the trench madness. The enemy is usually hidden in fortresses of concrete, barbed wire, and earth. The battlefield is seen as a ''huge, sleeping machine with innumerable eyes and ears and arms.'' Death is delivered by ''impersonal shells'' from distant machines; one is spared or obliterated by chance alone. The ''engines of war'' grind on relentlessly; the ''massacre mécanique'' knows no limits, gives no quarter. Men are reduced to ''slaves of machines'' or ''wheels [or cogs] in the great machinery of war.'' . . . War has become ''an industry of professionalized human slaughter,'' and technology is equated with tyranny.[2]

The subsequent downward course of this appraisal of scientific technology is well known. The development of atomic instruments of war has steadily altered the public estimation of science as an instrument of progress. First there was the great fireball and mushroom-shaped cloud over Alamogordo, followed three weeks later by the bomb that killed or fatally injured seventy-five thousand people in Hiroshima; thereafter was the Chernobyl disaster in the Soviet Union, followed by the gradual admission of the extent of the poisoned residues around the abandoned plutonium manufacturing center in Hanford, Washington; in our own day is the ongoing search, still in vain, for ''safe'' storage depots for nuclear waste; anticipated tomorrow is the marriage of nuclear weaponry and space platforms. And it is not only military uses that have changed the public's attitude. There is the adverse effects of technology on the quantity or quality of work and on daily life, matters to which we will devote some attention in our next chapter, while in the background, the cloning of genes threatens to invalidate the single most creative of all human acts, which is to perpetuate the species.

It is essential not to lose the point by overstating the case, for Today's appraisal of science and technology is not quite the opposite of Yesterday's. The difference is subtle but significant. What has changed is the degree of trust and the extent of hope that we invest in the scientific enterprise as a whole. Our brief review has intended to emphasize only that the assessment of the currents carrying us into Tomorrow includes an uneasy awareness that science can be the master as well as the servant of mankind, and that Carlyle's hopelessly old-fashioned concerns may be more, rather than less relevant today than when they were voiced. For the moment, it is enough that we recognize the unease itself as a new element in the shaping of our expectations today.

A second reason for the growing disquiet has more to do with the self-conception of science than with its real-world impact. In their early rise to social prominence in the flush of Yesterday's optimism, scientists largely regarded their task as a timeless, axiomatic pursuit that would enable them, in the words of philosopher Stephen Toulmin, "[to] decipher the 'language' in which the Book of Nature was 'written.'"[3] From this view—World War I being still far in the future—followed a widely shared conviction that science was a wholly benign means for the improvement of the human lot. This belief, in turn, expressed not only an infatuation with the marvels with which science was increasingly associated—the conquest of time, space, illness—but with the increasing conflation of science with the study of society itself. Auguste Comte in France, Herbert Spencer in England, and Lester F. Ward in the United States proudly claimed that the new field of sociology was a "science" of human behavior. Following suit, economics shed the self-description of political economy that had openly announced its social character from the days of Adam Smith through those of John Stuart Mill, and with Alfred Marshall's magisterial textbook published in 1890, adopted the neutral term "economics" for its investigations. In Marshall's *Principles of Economics,* geometrical diagrams and mathematical formulas, although tactfully relegated to footnotes and appendixes, soon became recognized as the core of the argument. Not least of the testimonials to the inspirational significance of science was its explicit appropriation by Marx and his followers. As Lenin wrote in 1899:

We base our faith entirely on Marx's theory; it was the first to transform socialism from a Utopia into a science, to give this science a firm foundation and to indicate the path which must be trodden in order further to develop this science and to elaborate it in all its details.[4]

The steadily widening and deepening presence of a science-centered social viewpoint is everywhere acknowleged today, but there is a difference in its evaluation. As we have seen, the shift is most immediately manifested in the growing unease with regard to the application of science to technology. But quite apart from that lies a less familiar change in the esteem that attaches to science from within its own ranks. The shift appears as a growing skepticism within the world of scientists with respect to the status of its self-generated knowledge. Until the 1950s and 1960s it was generally held that science represented the findings of a wholly disinterested inquiry into the nature of things—an inquiry whose conceptual premises and modes of advance rose above the influence of their historical context. The developing dissent from this view is intended not to dethrone science, but to recognize that human beings, not gods, sit on its throne; and that their conceptual starting points, methods of inquiry, and indeed visions of science itself are inescapably embedded in their respective historical contexts. Toulmin points out, for example, that Newton and his colleagues were not at all interested in the application of their discoveries to industry, but rather with their theological implications, and that many of their readers were concerned not with their implications for religion, but for politics and social structure.[5]

This more modest reevaluation of scientific knowledge has been a steady trend in the philosophy of science during the last few decades. In *The Structure of Scientific Revolutions,* published thirty years ago, Thomas Kuhn proposed the unsettling idea that far from existing in some empyrean realm, the ideas and theoretical structures of science represented ''paradigms''—conceptual structures whose premises and boundaries established limits, as well as foundations, for scientific beliefs.

From this viewpoint, science made its major advances by transcending the conceptions of an existing paradigm, rather than by exploring every implication of what was presumably the one-and-only true conception of whatever was out there. In *Philosophy and the Mirror of Nature,* Richard Rorty urged that philosophy abandon the idea of its mission as a search for a nonexistent truth, strongly suggested by the idea of the mind as a ''mirror,'' and turn instead to conceiving its task as an ongoing ''conversation'' about whatever matters it considered to be important. Perhaps most disconcerting of all was the assertion by the philosopher of science Paul Feyerabend that ''The only principle that does not inhibit [scientific] progress is: *anything goes.*''[6]

As part of this much more modest image of science, a chastening internal change has recently occurred with regard to the potential reach of scientific theory. Until a few years ago, a central ambition of science, at least among the community of nuclear physicists who constitute its vanguard, has been a unification of scientific theory capable of realizing Michael Faraday's conception of "Nature's seemingly distinct forces [as] but facets of a single, symmetrical jewel."[7] Even Stephen Hawking, one of its most thoughtful leaders, was so bold as to write in 1988 that "there is a good chance that the study of the early universe and the requirements of mathematical consistency will lead us to a complete unified theory within the lifetime of some of us who are around today, always presuming we don't blow ourselves up first."[8]

That hope is much less widely shared today than it was a decade ago. The immediate cause was a decision of Congress to cancel the funding for the Superconducting Super Collider, a key experimental device in the search for a unified theory. At first lamented by the physics community as spelling the end of a promising quest, in the judgment of many physicists today the demise of the collider may only have brought physics more quickly to an impasse inherent in its capabilities. As an article in the *Scientific American* pointed out, a collider capable of probing the "infinitesmal quantum gravity realm" would need to be capable of measuring effects in a realm that might be 1,000 light-years in circumference. The entire solar system is only one light-*day* around.[9]

Fittingly, it may have been Hawking himself who inadvertently supplied the *coup de grace* to his own hopes. At the conclusion of his earlier essay, he had written, "If we do discover a complete theory, it should in time be understandable in broad principle by everyone, not just a few scientists. Then we shall all, philosophers, scientists, and just ordinary people, be able to take part in the discussion of the question of why it is that we and the universe exist. If we find the answer to that, it would be the ultimate triumph of human reason—for then we should know the mind of God."[10] Thinking of the toy-sized universe that would be the product of a God with a mind no greater than that of "philosophers, scientists or just ordinary people," I am reminded of the title of a book of poems by Stanley Burnshaw: *Caged in an Animal's Mind*.

III

Let us turn next to capitalism, the force most directly responsible for having changed the age-old static conception of the future into the dynamic vision of Yesterday. As with the case of science and technology, important changes have introduced new, pessimistic elements into the outlook for capitalism Today, but here it may be best to begin with a positive rather than a negative change. This is the disappearance of the socialist challenge that to many constituted its single greatest enemy.

In its utopian forms in the mid-nineteenth century, socialism was never looked on as a serious threat to capitalism: when Marx was driven from Germany because of his revolutionary ideas, he was peacefully sequestered in England. Looking back, we can say that capitalism in those days perceived no real danger from an alternative economic system, because none existed. Even after the Russian Revolution of 1917, communism remained more of an ideological specter than a socioeconomic threat. Despite its rhetoric, in those days the most immediate and persistent source of anxi-

ety about capitalism's future sprang from the internal problems of the system, rather than from fears that it would be
bested by socialism, in whatever form. During the early
nineteenth century, for example, labor unions were widely
regarded as extremely dangerous institutions, and were sav-
agely treated, especially in Europe. Thereafter the concern
shifted to the threats posed by monopolies, a popular target
of the late nineteenth century in the United States. But by
the advent of the twentieth century, the most pressing source
of concern in all countries was perceived to be the instability
of the system itself, evidenced in constant worries over
"panics" and "slumps."

This concern reached a high point in the Great Depression, when national outputs plunged and unemployment
soared. In the United States, for instance, the gross national
product fell by almost 50 percent between 1929 and 1933,
while unemployment rose from just over 3 percent of the
labor force to just under 25 percent. At this point, socialism
finally emerged as a serious contender for an alternative
economic system. A socialistically-minded Popular Front
government was elected in France in 1936, socialist governments appeared in Austria and throughout Scandanavia,
Mussolini's fascist party openly declared its sympathy for
socialism, and Hitler's National Socialist Party incorporated
its name. Among the leading Western powers, only England
and the United States escaped a direct political challenge to
capitalism, the last by virtue of the charismatic leadership
and reformist program of Franklin Roosevelt whose New
Deal was in fact a mildly social-democratic movement in all
but name.

The outcome of the Second World War removed the

immediate fear that capitalism might succumb to a depression-induced change of regime, but the war also forced the new realization that Soviet socialism had not only become a mighty political force but was also capable of mounting a substantial industrial effort. Then, for the first time, socialism loomed as a credible alternative to capitalism. After 1947, despite a brief continuing official "alliance", actual relations between the United States, acting as the leader of the capitalist world, and the Soviets were warlike, using diplomatic, propagandistic, undercover, and limited military means, if we include mutual nuclear blackmail and contests over spheres of influence in Africa and Central and South America.

The conflict ended in the mid 1980s, with the increasingly evident economic breakdown of the Soviet system, an event that must be seen as playing a role with regard to the estimation of the future of capitalism even more critical than the altered view of science associated with the atom bomb, although of course in the opposite direction. The bomb changed the public's attitude toward science from trust to wariness, whereas the collapse of the Soviet system changed the view of capitalism from a mixture of enthusiasm and trepidation to a kind of acquiescence in its unchallenged hegemony. That change was much facilitated, of course, by various measures of social welfare that had been adopted in all capitalist nations to avoid the social consequences of another depression of the magnitude of that of the 1930s. But the crucial development with regard to economic expectations arose from the awareness that there was no longer a credible alternative to which to turn.

That is where things stand today. Ever since its postwar

reconstruction boom, capitalism has evidenced serious malfunctions in every nation. Unemployment in the Organization for Economic Cooperation and Development (OECD) countries since the 1970s has been running at levels not seen since the 1930s. In the United States, what economist Wallace Peterson calls a "silent depression" has descended upon the country.[11] By the early 1990s, the buying power of a typical worker's earnings was more than 15 percent *below* the level of fifteen years earlier. Real family income, despite the increase in the number of working wives, grew by only two-tenths of 1 percent, compared with 2.8 percent in the preceding quarter century. Over thirty-five million people, 40 percent of them children, today live in what has been defined as "absolute" poverty. Yet, throughout most of this long depression, conservative regimes have been firmly in the saddle, both in Europe and in the United States. In 1993 President Clinton came into office bringing hopes of a new New Deal, but no far-reaching program of social and economic change has materialized as of this writing.

There seems only one possible explanation for this sea-change of political sentiment. The political prospects for capitalism have been bolstered by the disappearance of its only economic opponent. Hence, in place of the long prewar leftward drift, there is now stasis. Indeed, if there is any political movement apparent in the West today it may well point in quite the opposite direction.

This appears to contradict my earlier thesis that the decisive difference between Yesterday and Today is the anxious state of our current expectations. Where can we discover the source of this anxiety if the threat of political

overthrow—inescapably the greatest enemy of any order—
has effectively disappeared?

Two answers suggest themselves. The first concerns
the prospects for overcoming the silent depression that has
undermined our economic health, giving rise to the suspicion that whereas socialism may have lost, it is not so clear
that capitalism has won. That problem affects Tomorrow,
and we will look into it in our next chapter. But a second
problem magnifies, and to a certain extent precedes, the
first. It concerns an aspect of the capitalist system that has
become increasingly apparent—and increasingly disquieting—in recent years. This is the relationship between capitalism's world-straddling economic framework and the political lines of demarcation that divide this framework into
national entities. In the conventional view of this relationship, a capitalist political world "contains" economies,
each of which fends for itself as best it can. But such a view
obscures another conception in which a capitalist economic
world contains political entities fending for themselves as
best they can. Thus our normal angle of political vision
leads us to overlook the lodgment of all national entities in a
global economic framework that enjoins on each and all of
them the successful accumulation of capital by their respective business systems.[12] The ensuing contest in the world
market probably determines the political fate of nations
more profoundly than anything but life-and-death military
conflict. We have but to call to mind the rise of England
to world power in the early nineteenth century and its relative decline at the end of that century, or the emergence of
the United States as a major political entity after the Civil
War and of Japan in the last quarter century, to appreciate

82

the importance of this continuous struggle for economic power and prestige.

That which invests this struggle with its significance for capitalism's future is the virtual exclusion of this all-important political contest from the direct responsibility or guidance of the state. As a consequence, nations rise and decline as the outcome of efforts carried out by individual firms, knit together into "economies" comprised essentially of unsupported and uncoordinated private units. There are, to be sure, exceptions to this generalization, such as the Franco-British Airbus or the complex interlocking of private management and public bureaucracy in Japan and in some of the newly industrializing Asian states. The fact remains, however, that national outcomes, even in these countries, remain very largely beyond government control. The wealth of individual nations, today as in Adam Smith's time, is determined in the first instance by the success of economic efforts, which in turn depend to a very great extent on the success of individual enterprises engaged in pursuit of their particular interests.

There has, nonetheless, been an important change since Adam Smith's time. The change involves the much-touted "globalization" of this private activity, meaning a dramatic internationalization of economic activity at every level of production and distribution. Thanks to advances in communication, transportation, and computation, one can supervise factory operations in Mexico with equal efficiency from offices in Chicago or Birmingham or Mexico City; one can bank in Djakarta with the same access to world capital markets as in New York; one can read memos written a continent away as quickly as those written downstairs.

As a result, economic activity that was once geographically bounded can now be located elsewhere. The immediate source of this change has been a dramatic rise in the number of "multinational" corporations—the United Nations Center on Transnationals estimates the increase from 7,000 such enterprises in 1970 to some 35,000 in 1991, the great bulk of the increase, incidentally, brought about by the hugely expanded use of multinational organization by medium-sized firms, not by giant multinational enterprises, such as General Motors or Toyota.

This intensified process of internationalization directly concerns the conflict we have already discussed between the generalized need for expansion of the capitalist order and the self-defeating outcome of that drive in a world divided into rivalrous political entities. In the last century, those tensions were eased through the division of the globe into a Center and a Periphery. The Center was located geographically in those regions in which the new capitalist order flourished—first in Western Europe, then in the United States. The Periphery comprised those areas of the globe in which capitalism failed to develop. During the period we have called Yesterday these "underdeveloped" economies gradually became servitors of the Center through the carving-out of well-demarcated spheres of influence—British India, the Belgian Congo, French Northern Africa, Japan-dominated Korea and Manchuria, and United States hegemony in Central and South America, the servitor in each case yielding cheap raw materials and protected local markets that its master needed to find a place in the world system.

Today things have changed—not so much in the Periphery where, despite brave talk of economic development, crushing poverty is still the rule, as in the Center, where the internationalization of economic life has made its greatest inroads. Older spheres of influence are of increasingly less importance as globalization encourages the interpenetration of neighboring markets, with ''world-straddling'' leaps whenever targets of opportunity open up. If there is any single conclusion to be drawn from this changing form of mutual rivalry, it is the inceasing ineffectiveness of national governments. As the sociologist Manuel Castells sums it up:

[T]he new economy is a global economy, in which capital, production, managment, markets, labor, information, and technology are organized across national boundaries. Although nation-states are still fundamental realities to be reckoned with in thinking about economic structures and processes, what is significant is that the unit of economic accounting, as well as the frame of reference for economic strategies, can no longer be the national economy. Competition is played out globally, not only by the multinational corporations, but also by small and medium size enterprises that connect directly or indirectly to the world market. . . . What is new, then, is not that international trade is an important component of the economy (in this sense, we can speak of a world economy since the seventeenth century), but that the national economy now works as a unit at the world level. . . . In this sense we are not only seeing a process of internationalization of the economy, but . . . the interpenetration of economic activity and national economies at the global level.[13]

Should this be cause for a more pessimistic outlook? To those who see the central drive of capitalism as essentially constructive, the change is likely to be interpreted as ushering in a new age, even a great new ''transformational'' boom of the kind that arises when socioeconomic maps change their configurations, and production-possibility curves move outward everywhere. Indeed, these days it is common to extoll the vitality of the market forces that drive the globalization process, and to decry the dead hand of political barriers that seek to dampen primal economic energies or to guide the direction in which they expend themselves. Economic globalization is therefore more likely to win friends than foes, as witness the general consensus among economists and business leaders in support of the North American Free Trade Agreement.

On the other hand, globalization will be greeted with less enthusiasm by others who see the diminution of national control as weakening the only means we possess to subordinate international private economic activity to the public interest. In particular, internationalization now intensifies the anxieties aroused by the poor economic performances of both Europe and America. For it poses the question of how the market will take care of the increasing number of Americans or Mexicans or citizens of any country who find themselves separated from employment because of greater market penetration across their borders. Thus, the growing presence of globalization raises the prospect of a world in which international economic forces—quite as impersonal as ''things''—are in the saddle and will ride mankind. I suspect that some such prospect, coupled with anxieties about our stubbornly depressed economic performance, accounts for much of the anxiety that, despite our unchallenged political hegemony, beclouds the economic future.

IV

We come finally to the belief in political emancipation as a force for progress. Here I shall be brief, but much less indeterminate than in the case of capitalism. Yesterday the political spirit appeared as the expression of the Rights of Man, bottled up for millennia, finally released to shape humanity's destiny. In very different voices, de Tocqueville, John Stuart Mill, and Walt Whitman were its inspiring celebrants; by contrast its critics appear to us as small-minded, defensive, ungenerous. As with science and capitalism, that current of history runs into the future, endowing it with a hope-filled aspect. It is true that some of the enthusiasm has vanished as democracy itself has become the chosen norm, scaled down to life-size by Churchill's famous denigrative affirmation of it as "the least bad form" of the unwelcome necessity of government. Yet the liberating political spirit continues to make itself felt in the West, generally in the steady enlargement of political goals to include civil, feminist, and sexual rights, despite the inevitable counterforces of fundamentalism, homophobia, and the like.

Matters are not so simple when the issues at stake involve the underlying economic prerogatives of Western society. All stratified orders—feudalisms, aristocracies, and centrally planned socialisms as well as capitalism—create privileged orderings from which flow the varied economic dispensations of dues, tithes, rents, perquisites, executive compensations, and market-derived profits. The acid test of the political will as a liberating force comes when it directs its democratizing energies against these economic dispensations—in the case of capitalism, seeking to make more equal the distribution of income and wealth, the balance of power between private and public spheres, the quality of life at the lower and upper ends of the scale.

Here the trend over the last century has been gradually in the direction of a more equitable division of income and wealth: for example, the share of total after-tax income going to the topmost 5 percent of American families fell from one third in 1929 to one sixth in the early 1980s, and the concentration of wealth also declined, although not so sharply, from the end of the nineteenth century until the 1970s. Over the last decade, however, this trend has slowed or turned around. During the 1980s, while the real income of most American families stagnated or fell, that of the top 1 percent increased by 115 percent. In even more striking contrast, while the numbers of individuals in poverty rose from 23 million to 35 million between 1975 and 1991, during roughly the same period the number of millionaires increased from 642 to 60,667.[14]

Thus the exercise of political will as an equalizing force in economic affairs seems to have come to a halt in our time, above all in the United States where managerial salaries average 100 times the average pay of employees, ten times greater than the ratios in other advanced capitalisms. Whether the egalitarian trend of the past will reassert itself we do not know. One of the problems of capitalism is that differences in income and property are allowed to exhibit disparities that would be considered intolerable, were they applied to political rights such as voting, or to civil rights such as equal access to the law. It is true that a historical perspective suggests that a modern political democracy is unlikely to acquiesce indefinitely in policies that constrict rather than expand the definition of citizenship rights. Hence, as long as the political spirit in the West continues to display its distaste for political and civic inequality, it is not unreasonable to hope that the tolerance of extreme economic inequality will sooner or later follow suit. Until that egalitarian spirit reveals itself, however, at least for observers like myself, it constitutes still one more cause of our current underlying malaise.

However inescapably uncertain the political outlook in the capitalist world, matters change out of all recognition when we look to noncapitalist parts of the world. There, vast new political energies have become unleased, but not in a direction that holds out at the possibility of a constructive resolution of tensions. In Adam Wildavsky's and Max Singer's "zones of turmoil"—Africa, much of Asia, South America, and Eastern Europe—it seems more realistic to agree with their expectation of a century, perhaps two centuries, of violence and disorder.

What Wildavsky and Singer do not spell out, however, is the nature of that turmoil and its all-too-possible repercussions on ourselves. The disruptive effects of the turbulent areas are not likely to manifest themselves in the spheres of science and technology, including war technology, or in the workings of capitalism. It is when it comes to political will that we find a much more threatening prospect. In a front-page story on ethnic wars a few years ago, the *New York Times* listed forty-eight trouble spots, including Basques, Normans, Alsations, Bavarians, Kurds, Puerto Ricans, Ossetians, Abkhasians, Catalonians, Tamils, Slovaks, Inkatha Zulus, Palestinians, Kurile Islanders—to which we can since add Rwandans and Burundis. Political scientist Benjamin Barber asks how "people without countries inhabiting nations they cannot call their own, trying to seal themselves off not just from others but from modernity and all its integrating forces [can be] be persuaded to subscribe to an artificial faith organized around abstract civic ideals or commercial markets."[15]

To Barber's description of latent tribal nationalism we must add the impact of modern means of communication, the Pied Pipers of our times. As Richard Barnet and John Cavanagh write: "Fantasies of affluence, freedom, and power flash across the earth as movie and TV images, offering the poor of the world a window into a fairy-tale world of money, thrills, and ease, but no door."[16] As a result, in the place of the grandeur of purpose that dignified the often bloody struggles of the past, a combination of tribalism and inchoate rage deprives the unleashed fury of the true *misérables* of the earth from finding any constructive focus. The assertion of popular will that was essentially boundary-making and order-bestowing in the eighteenth and nineteenth centuries becomes a force that brings only political anarchy and destructive institutional consequences. In the internecine struggles that have devoured much of the African continent, worked their havoc in the Balkans, emerged in gangster form in the former Soviet Union, and lie latent in India and uncertainly contained in the Middle East, the spirit of mass politics comes to resemble the rage of the ghetto, not the sustaining and constructive force of its predecessor in the period we call Yesterday—a time that has never arrived in most of the peripheral world.

Describing in horrifying detail the descent of areas of West Africa into a kind of Hobbesian "warre of each against

all,'' journalist Robert Kaplan foresees ''an epoch of theme-
less juxtapositions, in which the classificatory grid of
nation-states is going to be replaced by a jagged-glass pat-
tern of city-states, shanty-states, nebulous and anarchic re-
gionalisms.''[17] We cannot yet tell whether Kaplan's words
are prophetic, but I find important their emphasis on political unrest as the wild card in history's deck.

V

A last word seems necessary. The contrast between the outlook in the more horrendous areas of the world and that in
the quiescent West sheds light on more than the tragedy of
the zones of turmoil. It returns us to the theme of our present
chapter: to draw a plausible sketch of Today's vision as we
experience it. Here we can learn from the contrast we have
just emphasized between the role of political emancipation
in the zones of peace and those of turmoil. As we emphasized in our initial chapter, there are two aspects in which
Yesterday differed fundamentally from the preceding Distant Past. The first is that it introduced the notion of progress. The second is that its unique dynamism was not enjoyed by all societies.

For neither science, nor capitalism, nor political emancipation opened vistas for most of the world, as they did in
those relatively few areas in which these forces initially
appeared. The technology and science that entered the peripheral areas came there not as indigenous creations, but as
emplacements of foreign hegemony—the fortresses, if we
will, of economic empires. In similar fashion, the capitalism

that penetrated into the Periphery was exported from abroad rather than nurtured from within, and therefore served to constrict, not to liberate the forces of enterprise in the recipient areas. And most of all, political will manifested itself differently in the two zones. In the West it was the expression of previously ignored social classes seeking full membership in societies from which they felt unjustly excluded. In the South and East, metaphorically speaking, political will came as the desire to escape from the confinement of a foreign prison-state with which no sense of identity was shared.

All this bears on the reasons that the mood of Today in the advanced parts of the world is different from what it was Yesterday. The uncomprehending dismay, the vague guilt, and the intense anxiety aroused by the ravages in Africa one morning, Haiti the next, around the corner the day after, are not merely humanitarian responses to misery. They are uneasy reminders that dangerous appetites and propensities lurk below the surface of human affairs, unwelcome reminders of the limitations as well as the possibilities of the forces of progress. Not least it emphasizes both the uncertain reliability and the crucial importance of political will itself—of our capacity to intervene in, guide, resist, or simply to abandon ourselves to the currents of change that carry us into the future. The spectacle of the zones of turmoil brings home the realization that the zones of peace will also demand the exercise of political will in intelligent and humane fashion, and the capacity, however gained, to keep the darker forces of human nature from taking charge. These reflections lead us to the question that has surely brought the great majority of readers to look into this book in the first place—not the vision of Today, but the possibilities for Tomorrow.

5
TOMORROW

I

I must begin this last chapter with cautionary words. It is impossible to describe visions that will reflect conditions that have not yet come to pass. Accordingly, our task must be different from those of past chapters. Rather than projecting the shadow of Tomorrow's unknowable realities, I propose to ask whether it is *imaginable*—I stress this crucial word—to exercise effective control over the future-shaping forces of Today. This rescues us from the impossible attempt to predict the shape of Tomorrow, and leaves us with the somewhat less futile effort of inquiring into the possibilities of changing or controlling the trends of the present.

To be sure, in some ways this makes the present chapter an even more precarious undertaking than those that have preceded it. To begin, it presumes that the forces that have established the differences of Yesterday from the Distant Past, and that still shape Today's world, will continue to exercise their role Tomorrow. Hence, rather as in the case of the Distant Past, we are assuming that the conditions of the present will be the dominant realities of what is to come. More to the point, our task rests on the assumption that one can make reliable pronouncements about the feasibility of efforts to control the forces of change themselves. It goes without saying that this must be a rash assumption. Nonetheless, if we are to speak of things to come, it is impossible not to take the risk. Shaping the future will be closer to an imaginable possibility Tomorrow than at any previous time in history. An effort to write about visions of the future would be derelict if it did not venture opinions as to what can and cannot be done in that regard.

II

One last time we begin with science and technology, the source of two causes for unease as we look into the future. The first such cause is surely that we might use our ever-expanding technological capabilities to create weapons or products or industrial processes that will threaten the fabric of existence itself—environmental Hiroshimas on a vast scale—or that will give rise to interferences with nature of a kind that frighten us by their implications—the cloning of geniuses, the chemical fashioning of personality.

Here, there seems reason to offer at least some, not inconsiderable, reassurance. In our time there is no lack of an awareness on the part of both the scientific community and the government with regard to the dangers of nuclear testing, the fearful dimensions of the improper storage of nuclear wastes, or—at a less melodramatic but not less potentially dangerous level—the environmental impact of major engineering projects such as those carried out by the Army Corps of Engineers. Thus it is certainly imaginable that we will be able to avoid at least some of the more horrendous consequences of an unsupervised scientific technology, whether by professional self-monitoring or by government regulation.

The answer is less reassuring, however, when we turn to aspects of the problem that are transnational, and whose remedy would accordingly require effective international supervision or outright prohibition. At their worst, these threats include nuclear blackmail or various kinds, or what might be even more difficult to forestall, the buildup of the potential for such blackmail. Such an international nuclear discipline is not within today's grasp. Nor can we claim to have the means of halting the international dangers of technology in the form of environmental overload, primary among them global warming. In this case, the difficulty arises from the impossibility of confining heat-trapping carbon emissions within the nation that generates them. Thus, to improve the ambient temperatures in any one nation, it is necessary to curb the emissions in many nations. To ask even a prospering nation to reduce its pollution, very likely at the cost of reducing its rate of economic growth, would pose obvious difficulties; to ask it of a country seeking to escape from poverty would be tantamount to asking it to commit a kind of economic suicide—a demand that would likely lead to violent, perhaps even nuclear counterthreats.

Hence, it will be exceedingly difficult to exercise control over the dangerous international repercussions of science and technology. However, we are only asking whether it is possible to *imagine* an effective response to the dangers in question. Here the answer is less forbidding. It may strain credibility to foresee the exercise of international coopera-

97

tion needed to prevent a nuclear attack, and yet, if such an attack became imminent, its prevention, whether by diplomatic, economic, or even military means, does not seem beyond imagination. In the same way, if the discussion of global warming moved from forums of scientific discussion to excited public meetings around the world, it is not inconceivable to take action to forestall it—perhaps through a worldwide program of replacing carbon-generated power by wind or solar-driven means. That would, of course, entail vast transfers from the rich to the poor countries, but given the extreme seriousness of the situation this, too, moves within imaginable bounds.

There is, however, a second cause for unquiet in the prospect that science-cum-technology may radically debase the quality of life—nightmares of Charlie Chaplinesque assembly lines, or perhaps worse, assembly lines without need for the likes of Charlie Chaplin. This brings us to consider the impact of science and technology in the small, rather than in the large—small in the sense of a fallout of scientific technology, each element of trivial consequence compared with that of an atom bomb, and yet the fallout as a whole capable of converting a green field into an arid desert. The fallout takes the form of an array of artifacts, mechanical and electronic. Individually they have little effect, and indeed, often offer some small benefit, but collectively they radically alter the quality of life. In this altered world office workers ''communicate'' with invisible others by internets; shoppers and travelers and elevator passengers ''listen'' to music over which they have no control; users of the telephone who wish to speak to a particular person must first respond to recorded messages instructing them to ''press 1 if you are calling from a touch-tone telephone''; couples seeking an evening of entertainment are shown video "drama''; and young people "play'' interactive games against electronic devices. It is a world in which things are indeed in the saddle, riding mankind.

Can this intrusion of science and technology be bounded, confined to its needed applications, and kept from sucking the life out of our engagement with nature and with one another? I find that difficult to imagine. At its core, capitalism is a social order that marshalls and expends its energies in the pursuit of capital. Economists have differed over the source of that continuously pursued reward, but there is no doubt that expansion is the life process of the system. Without it, competition would continuously erode profits, and capitalists would find no incentive for investment. Thus, the commodification of life is not only an intrusion of science and technology into the tissues of sociality, but also the means by which a capitalist economy draws energy from its own environment.

A static economic society could certainly exist. It might prove the jumping off point for some kind of humane new social order, as well as for other, much less attractive means of handling the inescapable problem of the generation and distribution of income. But an economy without growth would be as incompatible with capitalism as a society without serfdom with feudalism. Thus Tomorrow may find ways of steering science-driven technology away from immediately threatening applications in capitalist societies, and may discover the means of asserting safeguards and bringing about international interventions, if the duress is sufficiently great. But halting its broad incursion into social life seems inconceivable, as long as capitalism exists. With its transient gains and its permanent losses, commodification is a necessity for a system that must expand to survive.

III

That conclusion leads naturally to what expectations can be formed as to the prospects of capitalism. Again, two judgments establish boundaries to our inquiry. We have already noted the first in our previous chapter: It is likely that capitalism will be the principal form of socioeconomic organization during the twenty-first century, at least for the advanced nations, because no blueprint exists for a viable successor. The attributes of various national capitalisms may differ considerably, one from another—let us not forget that a capitalist structure has underpinned a gamut of societies from social-democratic Sweden to early fascist Germany and Italy. But it seems plausible that all the imaginable capitalisms of the future will display the three characteristics that have established the identity of the social order in history: an extensive reliance on markets as the mechanism that guides private economic activity; the presence within society of two distinct realms—one reserved for governmental functions, the other for private economic activity; and energizing the whole, a dependency on the expansion of private capitals.

The second boundary-setting judgment is that capitalism will not last forever. Its internal dynamics are too powerful to permit us to imagine the system cruising into the future like a great unsinkable ship. The very essence of a capitalist order is change—technological change, social and political change, and economic change, as a glance backward in any capitalist nation will make unmistakably evident. To suppose that capitalism could last for millennia, as did the Incan, Chinese, or Egyptian empires, is to lose sight of the very quality that makes it a unique social formation in history.

Within the extremes of those two pronouncements, what more can be ventured? Let us begin by considering the problem that has increasingly plagued the system for the last hundred years—its ability to offer adequate employment through a satisfactory rate of economic growth. Is it imaginable that this long-standing difficulty could be overcome?

It may help clarify the problem if we begin by making a distinction between two kinds of economic growth—normal and transformational. The latter refers to growth that emerges when the production frontier is dramatically extended, usually by the technological advances that open vast new investment possibilities, such as the railroadization of the nineteenth century or the automobilization of the twentieth century. Such booms are highly employment-generating, but they come irregularly, and we do not know how to create them in their absence. Thus, whereas it is imaginable that new transformational changes will provide the system with its needed impetus during the coming century, it would be foolhardy in the extreme to count on such a fortuitous turn of affairs. Indeed, as we shall see, the current trend in technological advance points in a much less comforting direction.

By way of contrast, normal growth refers to the expansive properties of capitalism when businesses are pursuing their interests as best they can, without the stimulus of a visibly expanding production frontier. Growth of this kind typically fails to offer full employment. According to the studies of the Canadian economist John Cornwall, from 1920–1991—excluding the war years 1939–1949—the average annual rate of unemployment in Canada was 6.9 percent, in the United Kingdom 6.4 percent, and in the United States, 6.8 percent. Cornwall comments on his findings with regard to the United States that if full employment is defined as providing jobs for 97 percent of job seekers, ''then over a period covering three quarters of a century, [full employment] was achieved in only one year out of ten.''[1] If this level of performance continues, the most likely prospect for the future is one of inadequate, although not disastrous, unemployment, perhaps not a prospect to generate deep fears, but neither is it one to offer complacent expectations.

There remains, however, another aspect of the relation between technology and employment. It is that the very transformational technology that has boosted capitalist growth has done so by substituting high-productivity machines for lower-productivity human beings. Long before the age of the computer, machinery was systematically displacing labor in its most productive uses: In the United States, for example, agricultural employment which provided by far the main source of both output and work in the early nineteenth century, was the source of less than 3 percent of all jobs in the 1990s; manufacturing, the center of early twentieth century growth, offered less than one sixth of all jobs in the 1990s, compared with twice that in the

1920s, and by the year 2000 is projected to offer only 12 percent of nonagricultural employment.[2]

Because the main thrust of transformational technology is to create new industries, its positive employment effect will far outweigh its negative ones. But when no such promised land beckons, the negative aspects take priority over the positive ones. In the past the fear of technological displacement as a major difficulty of the system has generally been made light of by economists. In the early nineteenth century, for example, the famous English economist David Ricardo wrote that the population of a country was of no consequence provided that the nation's "real net income" remained the same. Simonde de Sismondi, a relatively little known French economic critic, replied: "Indeed? Wealth is everything, men absolutely nothing? . . . In truth then, there is nothing more to wish for than that the king, remaining alone on the island, by constantly turning a crank, might produce, through automata, all the output of England."[3]

The prospect of large-scale technological unemployment, long dismissed by the Ricardos and taken seriously only by the de Sismondis of the economic profession, may well have been overstated in an age in which machines were creating new employments more rapidly than they were eliminating old ones. But the fears of the past cast a longer shadow in an era in which automata have taken on physical and "intelligent" capabilities undreamt of earlier. Modern-day technology may well be transformational with respect to such matters as the location and organization of business, but it does not seem to carry expansive consequences for employment. The workless workplace is no doubt an exaggeration, but the possibility of a reduction in the need for labor comparable to that which has halved the number of manufacturing jobs in seventy years seems entirely within possibility. So does the likelihood that "high" technology will increasingly render redundant the supervisory tasks associated with middle managment, just as "low" technology did with the need for human performance of routine non-managerial tasks. It is hard to avoid the conclusion that the economic future poses a prospect of growing technological displacement.

Can we imagine a way of coping with such a threat? The question can be addressed from two perspectives: Do we possess the economic means to accomplish such a task, and are these means politically acceptable?

Considered as a self-contained problem, the challenge seems manageable enough. There is no great difficulty in designing policies that would effectively bring down unemployment, whether it arose from an absence of spontaneous growth or from technological displacement. The means would include reducing the supply of would-be employees by lengthening the period of education, advancing the age of retirement, shortening the work week and work day, expanding vacations and introducing educational sabbaticals, and encouraging employment-generating public projects on a major scale, from rebuilding the inner cities to community-based undertakings of many kinds.

Unfortunately, the economic problem is not self-contained. The more successful any one country's anti-unemployment program, the more likely that it will generate inflationary wage pressures as its labor markets "firm up." Given the ease with which enterprises can shift their operations elsewhere, these pressures would increase the movement of capital to countries that tolerated unemployment and enjoyed a lower inflation rate as a consequence.

Thus it seems difficult, in a globalized world economy, for any country, on its own, to institute an effective, long-run pro-employment policy. Is it then imaginable that international agreements might allow us to avoid this beggar-my-neighbor quandary? An international agreement to dampen the movement of capital to encourage employment-generating policies obviously goes against the general imperative of an expansion-minded capitalist world order. Yet, as with such threats as global warming, the imaginable is likely to reflect the urgency of the crisis. Levels of unemployment that are socially tolerable will probably not lead to international agreements aimed at encouraging employment, but unemployment levels that threaten social stability might do so. Once more, political considerations become the decisive factor in coping with economic problems, a consideration that returns us to the second of our perspectives on combatting the problem of joblessness.

This perspective brings to the fore a last aspect of capitalism's potential performance, arguably the most important of all. It concerns the use that can be made of the public sector. Here we should note, to begin, that in addition to tracking the rather dismal record of Canada, England, and the United States in combatting unemployment, Cornwall also recorded that of Sweden. The result was strikingly different. Whereas the United States suffered unemployment rates of over 6 percent in 26 years of the 1920–1991 span, Sweden experienced such rates in only 5 years. In fact, Sweden's unemployment rates rose above 3 percent in only 14 years of the period, whereas in the United States the comparable figure was 55 years.[4] Moreover, it is not only Sweden that has far outstripped the United States in controlling unemployment. Effective policies have been mounted in a number of European nations, such as Switzerland, Norway, and Austria, not to mention Japan, South Korea, Taiwan, and Singapore.[5]

The means by which this has been accomplished vary from one nation to the next, but in general all accept or encourage some kind of management–labor relationship that enables companies to resist slashing employment on the basis of short-run cost savings, and all approach the employment-sustaining use of the public sector as a pragmatic rather than political issue. By way of contrast, in the United States labor unions have been so seriously weakened during the last twenty-five years that there are no comparable arrangements concerning wages and employment; and public sector undertakings have been looked on with suspicion bordering on paranoia: the United States public sector provides a smaller proportion of total output than that of any other advanced nation—smaller by roughly one third compared with that of Germany or France, by 40-odd percent compared with the Scandanavian nations. Part of this, to be sure, reflects the absence, up to now, of a civilized public health program, the United States being the only advanced country unable to afford such a luxury for its citizens, although that absence is offset by the world's largest military sector, a burden willingly borne by the hegemon of capitalism.

Can we generalize from these conflicting experiences? I think they make plausible two very different long-term outcomes concerning the economic future. The first is a

gradual worsening of the level of performance in the capitalist world, brought about by rising levels of technological
unemployment. What may be the socio-political outcome of
such a deterioration is beyond any kind of reasoned anticipa-
tion, but the prospect is clearly not one to lessen the prevailing anxiety.[6]

A second plausible outcome points to the vision of a
more pragmatic and concerned capitalism, following policies that have succeeded in holding unemployment well below the level of social unrest. As we have seen, this will
probably require the creation of an international agreement
to protect these nations against destructive flights of capital,
whether among themselves or from outside economies.
Looking beyond the immediate issue of unemployment, it
also holds a possibility of capitalism moving toward a more
socialized structure, an outcome expected by such otherwise
widely dissimilar economic scenarists as John Stuart Mill
and Joseph Schumpeter. For Mill, the transformation would
bring into being a competitive economy managed by worker-
owned enterprises; for Schumpeter, a system whose large-
scale enterprises had become, in effect, civil-service organ-
zations. For all their differences, both were called by their
authors ''socialist.''

Would such socialized outcomes be compatible with
capitalism? This is tantamount to asking whether they would
still be largely coordinated by markets; retain a division into
a public and a private realm; and be driven by the imperative
of accumulation. It is the last that poses the crucial problem.
The essence of capitalism, as we have remarked more than
once, is its psychological and economic investment in the
continuous enlargement of capital, but that subservience

does not specify the size of the layer of profits, or the degree of income inequality, needed to remain "capitalist." The adaptive capabilities of capitalism vary greatly from one extreme of its gamut of contemporary realizations to the other. Some nations—I call again on my often-invoked Slightly Imaginary Sweden—may make a transition to a social-democratic capitalism with ease; others—it is impossible not to put All Too Imaginable America in this category—may not.

The political issue enters not only because adaptability varies, but because of the much more sobering fact that we do not know how to change whatever degree of malleability characterizes any given nation, including our own. Capitalism is not a system that is easy to steer under the best of conditions, and today's unsettling technological trends, increasing economic intertwinement and lack of international consensus on economic policy are certainly not the best of conditions. To be sure, if all capitalisms would adopt the most far-sighted policies, and campaign vigorously for international pacts that called for mutual competitive restraint, things might be very different. But the frustrating reality is that we do not know how to bring into being the political will necessary for such an effort. Especially in a county that has adopted the cowboy as its national social hero, it is very difficult to foresee the strong government-led and internationally coordinated initiatives that would, in all likelihood, be necessary to provide employment on the scale that is needed.

Thus, even though capitalism is today a social order without external challenge, military or political, it seems difficult to imagine that it will easily resolve the economic problems that spring from its nature and hover over its future. In these circumstances, the advocacy of measures that exceed the grasp of realistic imagination seems an exercise in piety. Better, perhaps, to answer the question of how to live with Today's economic anxieties with the admission that we must see what the political spirit makes possible. This was, after all, the country that once built the Panama Canal and brought into being the New Deal. Is it imaginable that we might use those selfsame capabilities to initiate a new kind of publicly led transformational boom? Within the compass of the foreseeable future, our economic prospects will hinge to an important degree on our estimate of that possibility.

IV

And so we turn once more to the political spirit—as before, not to predict that which is unpredictable, but to inquire into the imaginable limits of our capacity to bring the future under our control. It is already clear that expectations in this regard must be pessimistic. If our capacity for the redirection of our collective economic life is so limited and uncertain, despite the dependability of its central motivations and the clarity of its intended purposes, what can we expect with regard to the labile impulses, the vague specifications, of our collective political wills? Is there any basis for thinking that we can effect any taming of the ethnic, racist, and hypernationalist movements that are the expression of today's political temper in the zones of turmoil? Is there even an assurance that we can look with easy confidence to maintaining a safe course for democracy, the generally benign and moderate form of political life in the zones of peace?

I begin on this bleak note not to sound a call for resignation, but to clear our visions with respect to that which must be done. Looking to the zones of turmoil, the preconditions for constructive change are clear enough. The absolute first necessity is to overcome the horrendous poverty of the inhabitants of the shantytowns, barrios, and slums of Africa, Southeast Asia, the Near East, and Central and South America, where a billion people live on the equivalent of an American dollar a day, a standard of living that has no plausible economic meaning for ourselves, but whose political meaning is all too clear when we look at the faces that move across our TV screens.

Until that misery of life has been removed, not merely alleviated, it is delusive to expect that the political spirit of the underdeveloped world will find its normal expression in moderate voices, spelling out long-term, step-by-step programs of gradual "Westernization." The essential purpose of all politics of moderation is to safeguard the existing order of things. Such a patient and pragmatic spirit might perhaps develop if the rich nations were willing to make it a first order of business to modernize the economies of the poorer world—a course that would require very heavy taxation—and if the poorer nations took measures to stabilize their populations and to reduce the glaring disparity between their own rich and poor. As long as none of this is done, the political will of the world's underclass may appear quiet as an undisturbed lake, but it is a lake of gasoline.

Political prospects are certainly better in the advanced

world, although flammable ponds exist there too in their inner cities and neglected backwaters. Nonetheless, unlike the situation in the underdeveloped world, a substantial measure of economic and social progress is certainly imaginable within the near-term future in Europe and the United States. Slum life in Europe could very well be eradicated by a generation of heavy public investment, and is not beyond remedy in the United States, although the effort might require the threat of escalating violence before an all-out effort were made. But that is true, as we know, of many challenges. The crucial question remains the existence, manifest or latent, of the political will to address the problem.

Once again this brings us to the outlook for political life in the capitalist democracies—the adjective always to be stressed equally with the noun. Here individual predilections tend to shape the optimism or pessimism of our visions, but I would hazard the generalization that prospects for the political future are best grasped as extensions of the political past. That rule of the thumb suggests that the capitalist democracies will probably steer a conservative and cautious rather than a radical and bold course—a view that seems most closely to express the prevailing anxious and uncertain vision of these nations. Given the shortsightedness of the wisest among us, perhaps a politics of caution is best suited for ordinary times. But in the face of the strains and dysfunctions we have been examining, such politics may not be the best if we hope to alter that vision.

However disappointing, there is nothing further to be said. Mass political will, largely impotent during the Distant Past, has become the wild card of Today, and perhaps even more so of Tomorrow. Attempts to foretell its determinations probably reveal more about ourselves than about the citizenry whose wills we seek to foresee. Our political processes are inherently gambles on the moral capacities and socioeconomic understandings of the societies whence they emerge—thus the necessary stress on the capitalist nature of the societies we are wont to describe solely as democratic. Herein lies whatever light a book such as this may shed regarding our visions of the shape of things to come.

V

It is time for summing up.

Visions of the future express the ethos of their times, and we must remind ourselves, to begin, in the ways in which the visions of Today differ from those of the Distant Past. In the uncountable millennia that opened our overview two themes stood out. The first was the perception of the future as the product of the same forces—divine, natural, or man-made—that had produced the past. There was therefore nothing to be expected of the world of social relations, of collective good and bad fortune, of the shape of things to come, other than what had been experienced before. Accordingly, there was little incentive to speculate about, much less to plan for, a world different from the one at hand. The second theme was closely linked to the first. It was the belief that life would be continued after death. The seemingly universal need to deny our individual finality, in one form or another, was an Ariadne's thread visible throughout the otherwise so sharply differentiated attributes of human existence over the Distant Past.

Yesterday's 250-odd years represented a break with the perspective of the 100,000 year-long Distant Past, whose significance cannot be overestimated. The revolutionary change was the consequence of the joining of three previously nonexistent perceptions about the course of history— the idea of a scientific understanding that would force nature to yield up its secrets to man; the emergence of a mode of organizing production and distribution that would revolutionize the capacity of humankind to utilize nature's resources; and the appearance of an idea utterly absent from all the civilizations atop the great escarpment of civilization, namely the legitimacy of the will of the people as the source of their own collective direction.

Taken together the three forces formed the basis of an utterly new conception of the future as embodying Progress—that is, as ushering in with something like certainty, a future that would alter the condition of humankind in every dimension—power over nature, access to and expectations of improved material well-being, and political responsibility for its own fate. If religion lost much of its prominence in the eighteenth and nineteenth centuries, it is because Progress promised a kind of heaven on earth, if not during the lifetimes of its contemporaries, then in the existences of offspring who would embody their spirits.

In four respects Today stands in contrast to Yesterday. First, the future has regained some of the inscrutability it possessed during the Distant Past. Second, the marriage of science and technology has revealed dangerous and dehumanizing consequences that were only intuitively glimpsed, not yet experienced, by our forbears of Yesterday. Third, the new socioeconomic order proved to be less trustworthy than when it appeared during the late eighteenth and early nineteenth centuries. And last, the political spirit of liberation and self-determination has gradually lost its inspirational innocence. Hence the anxiety that is so palpable an aspect of Today, in sharp contrast with both the resignation of the Distant Past and the optimism of Yesterday.

As social historians, we might well bring things to a close here. But it is difficult to let go of our thematic narrative before it had been followed to the end. The desire to envision the future, as we have now remarked more than once, must itself be examined as carefully as that which it purports to show us. Moreover, when we examine the desire, the source of its urgency becomes plain enough. It reflects our need not to foretell what cannot be foretold, but to come to terms with that which it is impossible not to foretell—that in the end our society, our civilization, our very planet, and most important, our individual selves will come to an end.

This is, of course, where religion offers its consolatory visions, all of them ultimately addressed to calming the terror of death by holding out the promise of a life after death. Alas, for those of us who find these prospects unbearable— imagine enduring bliss eternally!—the consolations have no effect. It is to find some secular analgesic for what the theologian Paul Tillich called "existential anxiety" that people of like mind with myself seek to foresee the future. At a primal level it is simply to assure ourselves that human life will go on; at a more rational level, to depict its contours and design as best we can; and at a level that stands in for religious faith, to express what we hope for the life of humankind—the closest that we can come to a heaven on earth.

It is the last of these purposes to which we turn in these final pages. There are no assurances that life itself will go on indefinitely, not brought to an end by the predicted explosion of the sun some five (or is it seven?) billion years from now, or by horrendous wars and diseases, or by an act of global suicide—Jonestown on a worldwide scale, orchestrated through some universal television network of the future. Weirder things are imaginable.

Nor can anyone offer any plausible account of the course of events over the next hundred or two hundred years within the relatively orderly areas of the Western world, to say nothing of Africa, South and Central America, India, the Near East and elsewhere. I have stated my belief that a spectrum of capitalisms is the most probable political setting for the Western world over the coming of the next century, but that ultimately capitalism will exhaust its vitality, perhaps making way in some societies for a more egalitarian society and in others for more centralized and controlled ones. Beyond that vaguest of visions, I abjure speculating on the future in more detail. Any effort to foretell the course of politics, of social relations, of religious beliefs, or even of science itself over the next century is pure arrogance. We have no idea what the history books of the Distant Future will contain.

We must therefore address ourselves to the most poignant of the reasons that we look ahead—the desire to register our hopes for the very long-term prospects for humankind. This is an easily derided task, but one that strikes me as peculiarly suited to the conditions of our anxiety-ridden age. It is a vision that seeks to describe what might lie within the reach of humankind, if it succeeds in running the gamut of Tomorrow. If we prefer, we can call it a very general set of suppositions as to what a new level of civilization would require.*

We may content ourselves with three propositions, of which only the first is indisputable: humankind must achieve a secure terrestrial base for life. The earth must be lovingly maintained, not consumed nor otherwise despoiled. The atmosphere, the waters, and the fertility of the soil must be protected against poisoning of any kind from human activities. The population of the globe must be stabilized at levels easily accommodated to the earth's carrying capacity under technological and social conditions that we—and presumably, they—would find agreeable. Without such a stable foundation, there seems little chance to attain a level of civilization unmistakably more advanced than our own.

The attainment of such a civilizational advance is quite impossible today. It entails the absence of any socioeconomic order, whether called capitalist or other, whose continuance depends on ceaseless accumulation. No less

*In *The Shape of Things to Come,* published in 1933, H. G. Wells projects history into the twenty-second century in the form of notes that fall into the author's hands—notes taken in a dreamlike state by a person of great brilliance. The notes tell of a devastating war that rages from 1940 to 1950, destroying capitalist civilization and ushering in a Hobbesian condition of each against all, carried on with deadly means. World order is eventually restored under the aegis of a World Transport Organization, a distant relative of the Hanseatic League of the thirteenth and fifteenth centuries. Eventually a Modern World State takes shape, at first puritanical, gradually becoming humanistic. In the early twenty-second century, the State dissolves itself, making way for a liberated worldwide society that has passed beyond the need for nationalism, racism, and other such means of assuring order. Social life achieves new levels of cooperation and love. Longevity approaches the century mark, and death is as easily accepted as a welcome sleep. Individual property is no longer needed. Basic English becomes the lingua franca. The book is a marvel of insight, hindsight, and blindsight, in each category a lesson for those tempted to foretell the future.

does it depend on the elimination of the divide between the poverty-stricken and the wealthy regions of the globe. Such an elimination may be as wrenching and difficult as the scaling of the escarpment that separated prehistory from posthistory in the Distant Past, but until those living at the base of the plateau attain a quality of life comparable to that enjoyed on its heights, there will be no loftier plateau of civilization, only variants of the accomplishments and failures of our own.

The second prerequisite for civilizational advance is much more difficult to describe. It is to find ways of preserving the human community as a whole against its warlike proclivities. Two quite opposite extremes might achieve this end. The first is effective global government; the second is its abolition. Global government might indeed bring about peace, as might also a denationalized world of many independent settlements, villages, and communities. The community approach might seem more practicable if humanity had suffered fearful self-inflicted disasters that destroyed nation–states and left great areas uninhabitable. The world government approach seems more probable, assuming that no such holocaust has devastated the world, and that gradually a common second language and something like a common ''second culture'' provided the basis of a world citizenship, not unlike the Roman Republic. Neither ''model'' should be taken as a serious venture in political science fiction, but rather as imagined ways to reduce the likelihood or the extent of internecine national conflict—ways that must be found if the vision of a superior civilization is not to prove a mere chimera.

Is such a basis available? This brings us to the last of

our three prerequisites, namely that the Distant Future must be a time in which the respect for "human nature" is given the cultural and educational centrality it demands. What is meant in putting forward this treacherous phrase is an awareness of the complex role that unconscious drives and fantasies play in the determination of our behavior. This is not to say that such a general sensitivity will cause human nature to be "tamed"—the unconscious cannot be domesticated. But if we are to build a civilization that is recognizably more humane and decent than our own, it will assuredly require a citizenry aware of the hidden attractions of both power and submissiveness, of the fine line between rationality and paranoia, of the Janus-faced character of so many events and the dialectical and psychological unity of so many opposites. Only then will its inhabitants be able to choose, to judge and to act as wisely as it is in the capacity of humans to do. As I said earlier, this is an easily derided faith, but I must ask my critics if they have anything better to serve as our long-term goal.

Is a vision of a civilization unmistakably superior to our own beyond all imaginable grasp? It is certainly far beyond anything that can be attained Tomorrow, if we accept Singer's and Wildavsky's "a century from now, or perhaps two" as the timespan within which the "zones of turmoil" will more or less catch up with the "zones of peace." But we are not interested here in visions that may lie within Tomorrow's grasp. Our purpose is to project a conception of a shape of future things that lies much further ahead—a distant goal toward which humanity can travel only by long, slow, often errant marches, and whose particulars cannot in any way constitute more than a shimmer of light on the horizon, a half-imagined map of what might some day be our Land of Canaan. As such, its proposals are no more than the first tentative sketch of a social order whose lineaments will be a very long time in the making. Its utopian ambitions aim only at establishing a kind of secular afterlife, not for ourselves as individuals but as members of an extended family called humankind. Some such concept may become the sacral element that I believe it will also be necessary to cultivate within ourselves, if we are to pass beyond the contemporary horrors that attest, more than anything else, to its absence.

During this long, slow, and often errant march I think we can gain strength by reflecting on the Distant Past. For countless millennia humanity found the courage to persist, the inspiration to produce extraordinary works of art, the will to create remarkable civilizations, the strength to endure miseries, and the appetite to savor triumphs, all without the support of a vision of a living future that would be superior to the past. There is no reason why the same resilience should not support humankind if it now sets its sights on the Distant Tomorrow of our imagination.

It is enough that we can see the future as containing such imaginable possibilities. Openness and potential, without assurances of outcomes, are our substitutes for Yesterday's bright hopes for Progress and our consolations for Today's more knowing anxieties. These words may reflect easily trivialized sentiments, but I put them forward at the conclusion of this very short, extremely long survey of how the future has appeared and now appears, as a salutation to my fellow voyagers who wonder, along with myself, what humankind can accomplish.

NOTES

Preview

1. *The Wealth of Nations* (New York: Modern Library, 1937), pp. 734, 736.
2. Chatham. N.J.: Chatham Publishers, 1993.
3. Ibid., p. 3.
4. Ibid., p. 190.
5. See, e.g., Herman Kahn. *Things to Come,* with B. Bruce Briggs (New York: Macmillan, 1972); and *The Next 200 Years* (New York: Macmillan, 1978).
6. Ibid., p. xiii.

The Distant Past

1. Marvin Harris. *Our Kind* (New York: Harper & Row, 1989), p. 87.
2. Vernon L. Smith. "Hunting and Gathering Economies." *The New Palgrave Dictionary of Economics,* vol. II (New York: The Stockton Press, 1987), pp. 695–96, abbreviated. See also Marshall Sahlins. Chap. 1 in *Stone Age Economics* (New York: Aldine Publishing Co., 1972).
3. For descriptions of the Kalahari, see Elizabeth Marshall Thomas. *The Harmless People* (New York: Vintage Books, 1959), and Marjorie Shostak. *Nisa: The Life and Words of a !Kung Woman* (Cambridge, Mass.: Harvard University Press, 1981).

4. Henri Frankfort. *The Birth of Civilization in the Near East* (Garden City. N.Y.: Doubleday & Co., Inc., 1956), p. 9.

5. Samual Noah Kramer. *History Begins at Sumer* (Garden City. N.Y.: Doubleday & Co., Inc., 1959), p. 221. See also Carl Roebuck. *The World of Ancient Times* (New York: Scribner's, 1966).

6. Cf. Kramer. op. cit., pp. 200–203.

7. Morton H. Fried. *The Evolution of Political Society; An Essay in Political Anthropology* (New York: Random House, 1967), p. 35.

8. See Eric R. Wolf. *Peasants* (Englewood Cliffs. N.J.: Prentice-Hall, 1966), Chap. 1 and p. 78.

9. Karl Wittfogel. *Oriental Despotism,* (New Haven. Conn.: Yale University Press, 1957).

10. Michael Mann. *The Sources of Social Power: A History of Power From the Beginning to* A.D. *1760,* vol. I (New York: Cambridge University Press, 1986), pp. 39–40, 52–53, 67–69, 74–75, 97–98, 124, and passim.

11. Sahlins. op. cit., p. 37 (his italics).

12. Herodotus. *The Histories* (New York: Penguin, 1972), pp. 178–79.

13. Ramsay MacMullen. *Roman Social Relations: 50 B.C. to* A.D. *284* (New Haven. Conn.: Yale University Press, 1974), pp. 93–94.

14. M. Rostovtzeff. *The Social and Economic History of the Roman Empire,* vol. I (Oxford, England: Clarendon Press, 1957), p. 380.

15. Aristotle. "The Politics," in *Introduction to Aristotle.* ed. Richard McKeon (New York: Modern Library, 1992), p. 596.

16. Machiavelli. *The Prince and the Discourses,* Book Three, Chap. XLIII (New York: Carlton House), p. 530.

17. Robert N. Bellah. "Religious Evolution." *Reader in Comparative Religion.* 3rd ed. (New York: Harper & Row, 1972), p. 38.

18. Ibid., p. 41.

19. Plato. "Phaedo." *The Portable Plato* (New York: Penguin, 1978), pp. 272–73.

20. Ibid., p. 43.

21. Ibid., pp. 43, 44 (italics added).

22. Ibid., p. 38.

Yesterday

1. Condorcet. "Progrès de l'esprit humain," Introduction to *Époque* I (1795), from John Herman Randall. *The Making of the Modern Mind* (Boston: Houghton Mifflin, 1940), pp. 383–84. (Text slightly altered to correspond to the French.)

2. Joel Mokyr. *The Lever of Riches: Technological Creativity and Economic Progress* (New York: Oxford University Press, 1990), p. 167.

3. James George Frazer. *The Golden Bough* (New York: Macmillan, 1939), p. 49.

4. Mokyr. supra cit., pp. 224–38. For examples cited above, see pp. 217–19.

5. Michael Adas. *Machines as the Measure of Men: Science, Technology, and Ideologies of Western Dominance* (Ithaca, N.Y.: Cornell University Press, 1989), pp. 222–23. The quotation from Samuel Smiles is on p. 222.

6. Mann. op. cit., vol. II, p. 13; David Landes. *Prometheus Unbound* (New York: Cambridge University Press, 1969) p. 98.

7. William H. McNeill. *Past and Future* (Chicago: University of Chicago Press, 1954), p. 47.

8. Lewis Mumford. *The Condition of Man* (Orlando, Fla.: Harcourt Brace & Co., 1944), pp. 251–52.

9. Richard Cantillon. *Essai sur la nature du commerce en général'* translated by Henry Higgs (New York: Augustus M. Kelley, 1964), pp. 117, 119.

10. Karl Marx and Friedrich Engels. "The Communist Manifesto." *A Handbook of Marxism* (New York: Random House, 1935), p. 28.

11. Marx and Engels, op. cit., p. 29.

12. Smith, op. cit., p. 94.

13. *Wealth,* pp. 734–35.

14. Paul Mantoux. *The Industrial Revolution in the Eighteenth Century* (London, England: Jonathon Cape, 1952), p. 397.

15. Shepherd B. Clough. *The Rise and Fall of Civilization* (New York: Columbia University Press, 1957), p. 217.

16. Ernest Becker. *The Denial of Death* (New York: The Free Press, 1973), p. 127 (his italics).

17. Cited in Alexander Rustow, *Freedom and Domination* (Princeton, N.J.: Princeton University Press, 1980), p. 345 (author's italics).

18. Priscilla Robertson. *Revolutions of 1848: A Social History* (New York: Harper & Bros., 1960), p. 417.

19. Lynn Hunt. *Politics, Culture, and Class in the French Revolution,* (Berkeley, Calif.: University of California Press, 1984), pp. 15–16.

20. John Stuart Mill. *Principles of Political Economy, Collected Works,* vol. III (Toronto, Canada: University of Toronto Press, 1981), p. 754.

21. Alexis de Tocqueville. "Democracy in America," from Franklin L. Baumer. *Modern European Thought: Continuity and Change in Ideas* (New York: Macmillan, 1977), p. 315.

22. Baumer, op. cit., p. 392.

23. J. B. Bury. *The Idea of Progress* (New York: Macmillan, 1926), p. 346.

Today

1. Quoted in Leo Marx. *The Machine in the Garden* (New York: Oxford University Press, 1964), p. 178. See also pp. 177–78.

2. Adas, op. cit., p. 369.

3. Stephen Toulmin. *Cosmopolis* (New York, The Free Press, 1990), p. 154.

4. V. I. Lenin. "Our Programme." In Emile Burns (ed.), *A Handbook of Marxism* (New York, Random House, 1935), p. 571.

5. Toulmin. Ibid., p. 137.

6. See Thomas S. Kuhn, Supra cit. (Chicago: University of Chicago Press, 1962); Richard Rorty. Supra cit. (Princeton, N.J.: Princeton University Press, 1979), p. 378; and Paul Feyerabend. *Against Method* (London, Verso, 1975), p. 10.

7. John Horgan. "Particle metaphysics." *Scientific American* (February 1994): 97

8. Stephen Hawking. *A Brief History of Time* (New York: Bantam, 1988), p. 167.

9. John Horgan, op. cit. (February 1944), p. 98.

10. Hawking. ibid., p. 175.

11. Wallace Peterson. *Silent Depression* (New York: W.W. Norton, 1994), pp. 39–40, 135.

12. This approach generally follows Immanuel Wallerstein, *The Modern World-System* (New York: Academic Press, 3 vols., 1974, 1980, 1989). See also his "Crisis as transition" in *Dynamics of Global Crisis* (New York: Monthly Review Press, 1982), p. 13.

13. Manuel Castells. "The informational economy and the new international division of labor." In Martin Carnoy, et al. (eds.), *The New Global Economy in the Information Age* (University Park, Pa., Pennsylvania State University Press, 1993), pp. 18–19.

14. For after-tax income, see *Historical Statistics of the United States* (Washington, D.C., 1975), Series G. 342, and *Statistical Abstract of the United States*, 1988, p. 428; for wealth concentration, Paul R. Krugman, "The right, the rich, and the facts", *The American Prospect*, Fall 1992, p. 25; for the more recent rise in poverty, Lawrence Mishel and Jared Bernstein, *The State of Working America, 1992–1993* (Armonk, N.Y.: M. E. Sharpe, 1993), p. 274 Millionaire data reported in Derek Bok, *The Cost of Talent* (New York, Free Press, 1993), p. 104.

15. Benjamin R. Barber, "Global multiculturalism and the American experiment." *World Policy Journal* (Sept. 1993), p. 49.

16. Richard J. Barnet and John Cavanagh. *Global Dreams; Imperial Corporations and the New World Order.* (New York: Simon & Schuster, 1994), p. 419.

17. Robert Kaplan. "The coming anarchy." *The Atlantic Monthly* (February 1994): p. 72.

Tomorrow

1. John Cornwall. *Economic Breakdown and Recovery: Theory and Policy* (Armonk, N.Y.: M. E. Sharpe, 1994), p. 235.1

2. See Paul R. Krugman and Robert Z. Lawrence. "Trade, jobs, and wages," *Scientific American* (April 1994), pp. 45, 49.

3. J. C. L. Simonde de Sismondi. *New Principles of Economics,* Richard Hyse (ed.) (New Brunswick, N.J.: Transactions Publishers, 1991), p. 563n.

4. Cornwall. ibid.

5. See especially Charles R. Bean. "European unemployment: a survey, *Journal of Economic Literature* (June 1994): pp. 573ff. For Asian statistics, see *Yearbook of Labor Statistics,* International Labor Organization, Geneva, Switzerland, 1993.

6. See Edward Luttwak. "Why fascism is the wave of the future," *London Review of Books* (April 7, 1994): pp. 3–4.

Index